D0518136

FROM BIRTH TO BACKING

FROM BIRTH
TO BACKING

Give your young horse a head start in life by using the appropriate body
language, from the initial 'join-up' right through to early ridden work

RICHARD MAXWELL
with
JOHANNA SHARPLES

Trafalgar Square Publishing

First published in The United States of America in 1998 by
Trafalgar Square Publishing, North Pomfret, Vermont 05053

Printed in Italy by Milanostampa SpA

Photographs by Bob Atkins

ISBN 1-57076-120-5

Library of Congress Catalog Card Number: 98-84273

Copyright © Richard Maxwell & Johanna Sharples 1998

Richard Maxwell & Johanna Sharples have asserted their right
 to be identified as author of this work in accordance with the
Copyright, Designs & Patents Act, 1988.

All rights reserved. No part of this publication may be
reproduced, stored in a retrieval system, or transmitted, in any
form or by any means, electronic or mechanical, by photocopying,
recording or otherwise, without prior permission in writing from
the publisher.

Book design by Visual Image

CONTENTS

INTRODUCTION

In the wild, the horse is perfectly capable of looking after himself, and has done so extremely successfully for thousands of years. However, we have taken it upon ourselves to domesticate him and put him in an environment over which he has no control. We have taken away his freedom and assumed responsibility for his needs, and we demand that he serves us and performs to our command. Luckily he has forgiven us our arrogance, and once we earn the title of 'herd leader' in his eyes, his naturally generous and co-operative nature means that he will submit to our demands provided that they are reasonable, and will try his best to please.

But anyone who takes on the responsibility of a horse must pay as much attention to his mental as to his physical well-being, and good stable management reaches far beyond food, warmth and water: it involves an appreciation of his needs and an understanding of the natural instincts that guide his behaviour. A smart stable, new rugs and a pulled tail may gratify the owner, but an appropriate work programme, the freedom to relax by rolling in a muddy field and grazing with friends mean far more to the horse.

Since we have put him in a position where he can no longer look after himself, we owe it to the horse to make a good job of catering for these mental and physical needs. We must ensure that he is prepared for the job we expect him to do, and must be sympathetic and understanding as soon as he shows signs of reluctance. In my experience a horse will always

co-operate where he can, but like the rest of us, he will do so more readily if he enjoys what he is doing and respects the person who asks him to do it. If he suddenly starts being 'difficult' then there are invariably good reasons why he feels he cannot do as you ask, and he will be as upset about this as you are. Look for the root cause of the problem and you will find its solution.

While it is possible to reschool horses no matter what their age, their greatest learning curve is the period between birth and backing. After that, experience adds to their early lessons but does not materially change them. I hope this book will show you how to teach your horse those basic lessons so that he is properly prepared for life ahead. Even if you don't plan to keep the youngster, it is still only fair to give him a good start in life – a well mannered horse is less open to potential abuse and has a much better chance of finding a good home in the future.

Above all, remember that your horse will teach you far more than you can ever teach him, if only you are prepared to look, listen and learn.

Richard Maxwell

NOTE FROM THE AUTHORS

It is Richard Maxwell's personal preference not to wear protective clothing, as will be seen from the photographs in this book. However, we would always advise readers to do so when handling young horses.

THE BASICS OF BODY LANGUAGE

All ages

Before you can really understand another person and find out what makes them tick, you need to spend time observing and interacting with them. You need to know their likes and dislikes, their good and bad habits. You need to know how they behave socially, when they are off guard and relaxing with friends, as well as professionally, when they are at work. Gradually a pattern of behaviour will emerge and you will start to anticipate their reactions and to learn how they deal with certain situations; and with this knowledge comes an improved ability to handle and communicate with that person. So let's start by doing the same with the horse.

All good horsemen understand the importance of 'knowing' their horse, but this should go one step further than recording his resting pulse rate and buying his favourite food. Finding out about your horse, understanding his mind and appreciating his quirks are the keys to making him work willingly for you. A confident owner may well ignore their horse if he lays his ears back while they straighten his rugs or bring his

feed, for example, because they know from experience that he is making empty threats which mean nothing. A stranger may be a little more wary however, because to most people, a horse with its ears back suggests an aggressive nature. This belief may lead them to be aggressive in return, and adopt defensive handling techniques.

It is counter-productive to punish a horse for expressing himself, however, because to come down heavily on meaningless habits leaves no safety margin

▶ In both field and stable, take time to stand back and observe your horse. Who are his friends? Where does he stand in the pecking order? What is his self-imposed daily routine? How does he deal with outsiders?

for dealing with more serious ones should they occur. A true partnership with a horse of any age will come from adding what you know of his individual character to what you know to be true of the entire equine species, and treating the whole with respect. As with a person, you will learn most about the horse's character by watching him when he is relaxed, in those more private moments 'behind the scenes'. Observe his social habits: this is a good place to start gathering information which will later help you to train him. You need to know how he is viewed by others in the herd, so that you know if he is bossy or subservient, to guide your own reactions and help you make correct decisions later in his training. This is also a good reason never to keep a horse alone: it is in your best interests to nurture and encourage natural herd behaviour, and to use it to your advantage. For the complete picture you need to go back to the horse in the wild.

HERD BEHAVIOUR

Typically a herd of wild horses has a traditional family hierarchy consisting of mothers and toddlers, as well as teenagers too young to breed, a matriarch who runs the household and a father figure who distances himself from the domestic scene. A herd is headed by the stallion, with five to twelve mares with their current foals at foot, plus yearlings and older fillies who have not yet started breeding. Ecology ensures that there is not too much inbreeding because only the strongest stallions in their prime will have their own herd, and any

weak offspring will fall prey to predators. The colts aged two years and over are driven out by the stallion and hang around in groups, fighting amongst themselves, building up their strength and awaiting a chance to assert their challenge for leadership of a herd.

The dominant mare deals with the day-to-day running of the group and is responsible for discipline within the herd. She is chief housekeeper, wife, mother and schoolmistress. There is no question of 'wait until your father gets home' – she has absolute control and the youngsters know it. If anyone gets cheeky she will single out the offender and send him away from the rest of the herd with aggressive body language, so he is temporarily outlawed for bad behaviour, like a child which has been sent to his room. The difference is that for a horse in the wild there is safety in numbers, so if this naughty child doesn't watch his manners, he could, whilst out on his own, be attacked and eaten. The incentive to return to favour is therefore extremely strong! The dominant mare looks out for signs of remorse and submissive behaviour, and only when she feels the sinner is sufficiently apologetic will she allow him to return.

The idea that the herd is a 'comfort' zone and that 'company' equals 'safety' is the essence of the handling methods passed on to me by Californian trainer Monty Roberts. This form of natural discipline is the basis of the methods you should use to train your youngster from day one, and it is so ingrained in the equine psyche that it can also be used to reschool the older horse safely and effectively. The reason these methods work so much more quickly and effectively than conventional ones is because even with a previously unhandled horse, you are halfway there before you even start work – you merely repeat what thousands of years of instinct have already taught the horse, talking to him in a language which he already understands. Making the horse see you as the substitute 'herd' or comfort zone to which he wants to return is all-important, whether you are halter-breaking the young foal or dealing with behavioural problems in an older horse. Every time I take a horse of any age into the round pen to start work (see Stage 6), it confirms that this method of natural discipline works.

AGGRESSIVE

A dominant horse may use the following signs to send another horse away from the group – ears flat back, mouth and muzzle tight, teeth bared, tail high, nostrils flared, direct eye contact and square posture, and he will advance towards it.

SUBMISSIVE

The offender will lick and chew, lower his head and neck, and 'hoover' the ground; he will register the importance of the dominant horse by locking the inside ear onto him, but will not make direct eye contact, and will retreat away from it.

PASSIVE

The following signs are typical of a passive attitude: ears softly back or flopped to the side, 'dozy' eyes and softness around the muscles of the mouth and muzzle, a floppy lower lip, resting a hind limb, and the tail

FIGHT OR FLIGHT

The horse's small stomach is prone to colic and impactions if it does not receive constant roughage and several small feeds a day (contrary to popular belief, it was not specially developed to complicate the life of the horse owner!). This is because, as a flight

▲ The horse's entire physiology is a testament to its existence as a flight animal

▶ Your horse should be completely comfortable and trusting in your company

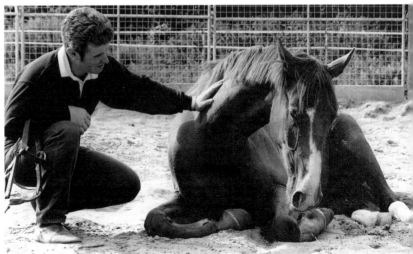

animal, the horse simply cannot risk being caught with a full tummy to slow him down – for instance, if a marauding lion happens to approach. The horse's mobile ears, his all-round sight, large nostrils and sensitive skin alert him to the slightest change in his environment. With this in view, ask yourself then why a whip or spurs should ever be necessary on a horse – he is designed as a hypersensitive being, and if he can feel a fly landing on his skin, he can certainly feel the pressure of the subtlest aid from his rider.

At any point in the course of a twenty-four-hour day, for seven days a week, twelve months a year, the wild horse must be ready to run for his life. Only in extreme circumstances, when his life is threatened and he is completely trapped, will he fall back on the second option which is to turn and fight. It is extremely unusual to find any horse which is genuinely aggressive or threatening by nature, and in such cases you should dig deeper to find the true cause of this behaviour, rather than punishing it and driving the horse to an even more defensive attitude.

Human physiology testifies that we are predators, and in some continents horse meat is on the menu along with all the rest. Our teeth and intestines are

► Part of our responsibility is to allow the horse to express normal behaviour as far as possible, even though most are kept in a highly abnormal situation

► Horses are naturally gregarious and appreciate company of any kind

designed to process meat, we have eyes on the front of our head, and we are not built for speed in the same way as a flight animal. When you are out riding it is possible to get very close to deer or other wildlife because as long as you are on horseback, you don't look like a predator. When you are standing on your own two feet or out walking, however, you are instantly recognisable as a predator and it is highly likely that any deer will see you and run off long before you see them.

This is the mentality which every horse born into domesticity has to overcome, so be patient. You are asking him to ignore the fact that you look exactly like the predator his instincts tell him to avoid; not only that, you want to handle him, and you want him to allow you to cling to his back in exactly the same way that he associates with being attacked and brought down by a big cat in the wild. It's a lot to ask.

UNDERSTANDING FEAR

Horses think like horses, not like humans, and when in doubt they will naturally revert to their programmed 'flight' instinct. Thus, when a quick reaction is called for, the body doesn't have time to send a message to the conscious part of the brain, ask for an opinion, weigh up the odds, decide how best to react and organise the necessary resources such as a faster heart and respiration rate! All this happens naturally whether the fear is real or imaginary, and with the heightened

perception of a flight animal, domestic horses remain at the mercy of their instincts to a varying degree throughout their lives.

In the words of the old adage, 'familiarity breeds contempt', and a certain amount of 'desensitising' is possible which will make the life of the domestic horse altogether less scary. By being exposed to his fears as much as possible, the horse will eventually realise that he is facing them *and surviving*, and the deeply ingrained flight instinct will be slowly broken down. This is one of the aims of training any young horse, and is explained in more detail in later stages.

STABLE MANAGEMENT

In natural conditions the herd will graze over an area of up to thirty square miles, so wild horses are unlikely to suffer from any of the problems which commonly plague their domestic relatives: worms, obesity, joint problems, overgrown feet or sheer boredom. The wild horse doesn't develop what we call 'vices' because he gets plenty of exercise, a constant change of scene and an appropriate diet.

For his own health and sanity, a horse should be turned out in as big a space as possible every day, come rain or shine. He should also have company, and horse

▲ Actions speak louder than words, as every horse knows. As a herd animal, he must keep a close eye on what's being said by his fellow equines as they graze in the wild. After all, it's the difference between life and death, and although your average horse is highly unlikely to be attacked by marauding wolves in his paddock or livery yard these days, instinct doesn't stop him worrying about it anyway!

owners should do their very best to give their animals the freedom to graze in company for several hours a day. This is especially important for youngsters who will take their first lessons in discipline from other equines, and so develop a healthy respect for the system of herd hierarchy. Bear in mind you will use this same system later to train your youngster, so the earlier his exposure to it, the better.

In a natural state wild horses have an endless supply of fibre of comparatively low nutritional value, and living on this keeps their teeth adequately worn down and their weight constant, and their gut healthy, since their digestive system is designed to assimilate to best advantage a constant input of low-grade fuel. As most humans know, or at least suspect, a fit and healthy body goes a long way towards maintaining a happy and contented mind.

TALKING HORSES

Whatever his breed, background or situation, the horse's understanding of the rules governing the wild herd still apply. Every horse, wild or domestic, communicates in the same simple and highly visual way, as you will have seen during your observation of horses at grass. Most horses will learn a few key words such as 'halt' or 'walk on', but all too often we create problems because we fail to communicate effectively with our horse, and then punish him for what we call 'disobedience'. His surprise at our unreasonable treatment of him leads to frustration and resentment, and both horse and rider soon find themselves in a vicious circle of misunderstanding. So rather than trying to teach the horse your language, why not meet him halfway by learning some of his? Not only will you get your message across more quickly, but you will also be able to interpret his response and have a two-way conversation, even if you are not quite 'word perfect'! Consequently, training takes half the time and is doubly effective.

Think back to how the horse learns his lessons in the wild, then translate it to the domestic situation. Thus a horse may behave aggressively – for instance a dominant horse may use the following signs to send another horse away from the group: ears flat back, mouth and muzzle tight, teeth bared, tail high, nostrils flared, direct eye contact and a square posture, and he will advance in a threatening manner. Or he may be submissive: he will lick and chew, lower his head and neck, 'hoover' the ground, register the importance of the dominant horse by locking the inside ear onto him but without making direct eye contact, and he will retreat from the more dominant individual.

BODY LANGUAGE

Despite years of domestication, every horse still understands the language of 'equus' and will react as nature intended as far as possible. Most of the behaviour which humans perceive as problematic is in fact purely instinctive: the horse's strong sense of self-preservation tells him to bolt from any situation in which he feels insecure, or to shy at an object which appears threatening. He can't stop himself doing it any more than you can prevent yourself from jumping when someone unexpectedly lays a hand on your shoulder. The same sense of self-preservation tells the horse that there is safety in numbers, so as a 'flight' rather than a 'fight' animal, he is instinctively programmed to make friends and seek company wherever possible.

As the horse's handler, you can exploit this instinctive desire. By imitating his natural body language you can communicate effectively with the horse, offering friendship or putting him in his place in spite of the fact that you are a different species. Imagine you are struggling to communicate in a foreign country. You need to ask for directions and are subconsciously looking for someone whose expression and demeanour suggest that they will be helpful and friendly. You look for passive body language – and so does your horse when he is deciding if someone is a friend or foe. Likewise there will be others whose aggressive body language suggests hostility, and this will deter you from approaching – just as your actions could unwittingly deter your horse.

HOW DO I DISCIPLINE MY YOUNGSTER?

Cute they may be, but foals are also extremely strong and grow more so by the day, so it is important that they remember that you are above them in the herd hierarchy. There is no need to be boring by reminding a foal of this constantly, but when he *does* overstep the mark, you must deal with any lapses in respect immediately. The most effective way to do this is in the same way as another horse would discipline a cheeky youngster – with body language and threats rather than actual physical abuse. This way there can be no excuses or misunderstanding; your youngster will understand what you are saying to him because you are speaking his own language.

Apart from being the clearest way to communicate displeasure to your horse, body language has other advantages over physical punishment: if you raise your hand or smack your youngster with a whip, you are storing up problems for later in life, because one day you will need to raise that same hand to put on the horse's bridle or stroke his face, or use that whip as a schooling aid to encourage more impulsion and energy – and how is the horse supposed to know the difference? He must never see your hands as instruments of punishment or torture. Instead, take up the aggressive stance pictured and make a naughty youngster feel intimidated and uncomfortable by invading his personal space, just as the dominant mare in a herd would.

PERSONAL SPACE

We all have a bubble of air around us which is invisibly marked 'by invitation only'! You may not mind family and close friends entering this space, for example to hug you or whisper something in your ear, but if some acquaintance or worse, a complete stranger, does the same, you feel annoyed and uncomfortable. You instinctively back away from them even if they haven't actually touched you, because you perceive their manner to be threatening and aggressive.

Horses are extremely aware of the idea of personal space, and adopting this behaviour is an excellent way to discipline them without raising a hand. Make direct eye contact, square your shoulders and march into their personal space until they back off, avert their eyes and begin to lick and chew as signs of submission. Imagine you are marching into a shop to complain about

◄ My aggressive stance: the shoulders are square and directly facing the horse, there is direct eye contact and the whole effect is that of supremacy and confidence. As a flight animal, the horse is made uncomfortable by confrontation, and such body language can be used to assert your authority

▼ Without actually making contact, the chestnut horse is clearly putting the grey in his place. This is the equine equivalent of my 'aggressive' stance

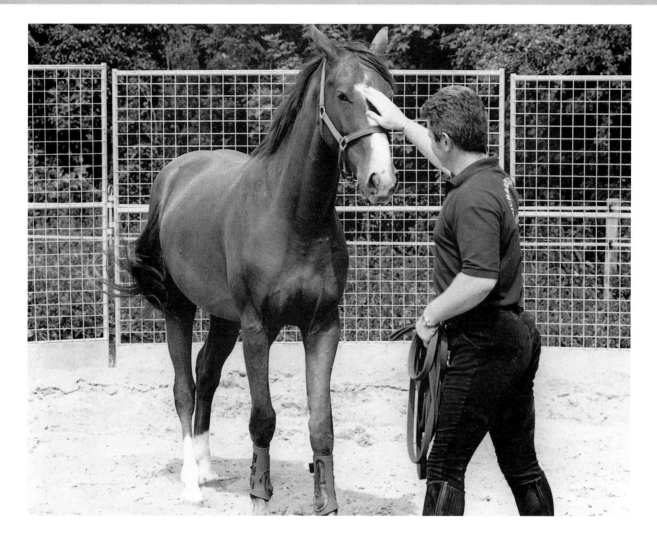

▲ A rub between the eyes is my usual form of rewarding a horse. Titbits are not recommended

something that has really annoyed you and to demand your money back!

If you aren't convinced, think of horses in a field sorting out the pecking order: they appear to bite and kick, but in reality make little contact and rarely injure each other. There is strength in numbers, remember, and while they want to keep a strict hierarchy they don't want members of their family falling by the wayside with fatal injuries – that would be in nobody's best interests! Dominant horses will graze happily with others provided that these keep their distance. There appears to be a magical line which must not be crossed; thus horses will happily share the same field, but if a less dominant horse wanders too close, the others are immediately aware of it and tell the upstart to keep its distance by using threatening gestures. As further proof of the horse's awareness of personal space, think of the herd which has been startled: all the

horses will swing round at exactly the same moment and set off at a gallop in a completely organised group, with never a crash to be seen!

Until your youngster is schooled to respect you and your space you may have to stamp your feet or even wave your arms to get the message across. However, like all schooling methods, this one will become refined with use until you can discipline your horse with the mere suggestion of an aggressive stance. Without raising a hand you can clearly say, 'Back off, mind your manners and have some respect'.

HOW DO I REWARD MY YOUNGSTER?

For every negative there must be a positive, so if you are going to discipline a horse when he is cheeky he must also understand that positive behaviour is rewarded. By reward, I do not mean treats and titbits: the reward your horse should value above all others is your companionship and good opinion.

If you are pleased with your horse's behaviour you do the opposite of what is described above. You invite him into your personal space as a special treat by using a soft, rounded posture. When he has submitted, repented and come close to you, speak softly to him and rub him between the eyes or scratch his neck as a reward. This 'mutual grooming' ritual is what his friends and equals in the herd would do; it takes the pressure off him and makes it clear that you are only bossy and demanding when he pushes his luck! If he is prepared to listen and behave, then you are prepared to drop the superior attitude and be friendly. You will be surprised how quickly your horse works this out and increasingly seeks positive reward and the 'comfort zone', rather than the negative effects which bad behaviour incur.

STAGE 1
CHECKPOINTS

- Observe your horse in a herd situation and learn what type of character he is.

- If you want your horse to be well behaved, keep him in as natural a situation as possible – company and daily turnout are essential.

- When handling a horse, give due respect to his natural flight instincts.

- Make sure that *you* are at the top of the hierarchy, and maintain a balance of respect without fear.

- Ensure that your horse enjoys your company. For successful training, he must see you as a 'comfort zone'.

- Dig deep to find the root of problems before they escalate. Horses are never aggressive by nature, but may appear defensive through fear, pain or misunderstanding.

- Remember that you are the predator. The horse will not trust you automatically, his trust must be earned.

- Check your own body language when handling your horse, and tune yourself into his.

- The horse must appreciate your personal space and stay out of it from day one.

- Desensitising the flight animal to help him cope with domestic life is the key to successful training.

▲ My passive stance: a soft, rounded posture, presenting the back to the horse and avoiding direct eye contact, will be perceived as non-threatening. Use this to instil confidence in a horse, especially when approaching him in the field or stable

EARLY LEARNING

Age: 0–6 weeks

A foal is born effectively as a wild animal, with all the instincts it needs to survive still unharmed. If that foal is destined for life as a working, domestic animal, those instincts may be controlled but they must be respected. The better he is trained to accept the daily demands placed on him, the more he will enjoy the company of the humans who will play such a big role in his life. Each horse is able to suppress his wild instincts to a different level: some become 'bomb proof', others will remain hypersensitive to their environment. If you know your horse's optimum level of sensitivity you will find it easier to judge his behaviour and to react accordingly: you will know if it is best to praise or discipline him, push him further or back off. Taking the most appropriate action when handling a young horse is not so much a matter of experience, as observation: if you observe the horse and take note of what his body language tells you, you are likely to see problems coming and to nip them in the bud. Be sympathetic without being soft, interpret the signs your horse is giving you and act on them. A good first impression that earns the foal's respect without adversely affecting his confidence, will set a good foundation for a lifetime of training.

SURVIVAL OF THE FITTEST

In the wild, herd safety depends on having a strong leader. In a domestic situation this leader is you, and it is natural that your authority will occasionally be challenged. In fact the more talented and intelligent a horse is, the more difficult and precocious he can be to handle. Those with the ability to reach the top may challenge and question you every step of the way, and if you fail to rise to that challenge or answer his questions satisfactorily, you will lose their respect. Handled badly, a simple misunderstanding between horse and human might escalate into a full blown argument, and put your whole relationship in jeopardy. Handled well, mistakes are a vital part of the young horse's learning process and can actually strengthen the bond of trust and respect between you. Whether the young horse views the human/equine relationship with confidence and curiosity, or fear and insecurity, is up to the handler. The young horse is a blank page, and it is you who will dictate what is written there.

Remember that your foal knows nothing of life and must always be given the benefit of the doubt in his early training. He may have seen humans around and become used to their presence since birth, but he has no concept of what they expect of him or what their role in his life will be. Unlike older horses which may be deliberately testing you or trying to make a point, most foals have not yet reached that stage of guile, so if they refuse to do as they are asked it is far more likely to be because they are afraid, or don't understand what you want.

If you are too severe in your reactions to an unco-operative foal, he is more likely to panic than to start doing as you ask, and you can forget lessons for the day. Like a frightened or hysterical child, the foal will become even less co-operative and more convinced that his paranoia is justified! Rather than viewing such a moment as detrimental to your relationship however, welcome it as an opportunity to reassure him and win him over as your friend every time he has doubts. Be his 'friend in need' and he may well return the favour should you make a mistake in his handling much later, perhaps during the more complicated backing or schooling process. Now is the time to establish his confidence and win his trust, and this will stand you in good stead when you begin riding him later on – it is vital that when you say, 'It's OK, trust me...' at a later stage in his training, your youngster has every reason to believe you.

IMPRINTING

WHAT IS IMPRINTING?

Immediately after a normal birth there is a period of approximately one hour before the foal struggles to his feet. In this time he will bond with his mother and other herd members, and take in all the sights, sounds and smells of his new universe. This is known as the imprinting period, when he is most acutely receptive to outside influences and learns how to react to them, a conditioning process which may prove vital for his survival in the wild. If you are lucky enough to be present when your foal is born, you are in a position to take advantage of this most influential moment in his life.

This intensive learning period takes place in every young animal's life but at a different time according to the species. The young of predatory animals such as humans, wild cats and dogs are born helpless and often blind, and are extremely vulnerable for several weeks, if not months, after birth, relying entirely on their parents to provide for and protect them. As they become more robust and mobile, they observe and learn from their parents to an increasing degree until they are capable of looking after themselves. The foal is not ignorant and vulnerable in the same way as these babies, however – he has the reactions of an adult horse, but is just lacking their experience. Thus his survival will depend upon him being a quick learner, and the imprinting process described below takes full advantage of this.

At the moment of birth, the domestic foal doesn't know that his life is going to be any different to that of his wild ancestors. He is born expecting to flee in order to escape danger, and is instinctively programmed to run from predators. Normally you, as a human being, would be included in this category, but if you make your presence felt during that initial bonding period after birth, the new-born foal will accept your touch and presence in the same way that he accepts those of his mother, despite your obvious predatorial characteristics (see Stage 1). Just as the foal will later recognise

his mother by sight, sound and smell in a crowd of hundreds, you will be 'imprinted' in his memory and he will remember that *you* mean something important to him, too.

WHY IMPRINT?

If the foal is to grow into a contented and well trained domestic horse, his acceptance of humans must be total, and he should never succumb to his instinctive desire to run away from them. Foals do not bond with humans automatically, as can be seen from the many foals running about which see humans every day of their lives but are still wild and unruly. Moreover brief daily handling from humans is still not enough to outweigh the thousands of years of evolutionary conditioning which tell the foal that here is a predator.

Imprinting takes every-day handling one step further, its objective being to override the foal's flight instinct and to 'desensitise' him to the touch of the 'predator' – the human – who will ultimately be his

◀▶ Because the horse is a flight animal and may have to run for his life at any moment, the foal's mind and senses have to be fully developed at birth even though he may not be fully developed physically

rider and companion. Many people believe they should withdraw quietly and leave the mare and foal alone after the birth, but in fact this does not make the foal's life any easier in the long run. Imprinting has been given great credibility in the United States, where certain stud vets find that foals who needed their assistance at birth are consistently more friendly and easier to handle later in life than those which enjoyed a trouble-free birth, but therefore without any contact with people. The true effects of imprinting may not become apparent until later in the foal's life when, as long as the imprinting experience has been favourable, he will accept the things we do to him, such as putting on a saddle or administering a worming syringe, with far less argument than a foal which has not been imprinted.

It goes without saying that the first impression you 'imprint' on the foal must be a good one, and that you must take the opportunity of meeting him, and teaching him that he should have no fear of you, when he is at his most vulnerable and receptive; ideally, this is within the first hour of birth. You may be usurping the natural sequence of events by influencing the foal before he is completely sure what is going on, but it is entirely in his best interests. It is the responsibility of all those who handle young horses to make things as clear and

pleasurable as possible for them, and a little time spent imprinting a foal with the human touch at this moment in his life will save a great deal of stress, time and possibly injury to horse or handler later on. When the time comes for riding him, the imprinted foal definitely has a head start, and it is much easier to spend half an hour or so introducing the foal to the basics of his relationship with humans while he is smaller and weaker than you and has no alternative ideas, than to attempt it for the first time with a fully grown horse.

How Do I Imprint?

The best time to imprint a foal destined to be a domestic animal is as he lies on the ground waiting for the strength and circulation to get through to his young legs, in the first hour or so after birth. The imprinting process may start even earlier if there are difficulties with the birth, but in most cases the foal's first introduction to humans will be as he is rubbed down with a clean towel or straw afterwards.

Once this has been done, kneel down beside the foal and start working over his face and head with small rubbing motions. Move all around his eyes, over and into his mouth, rubbing the lips and gums, and around and inside each ear and nostril. The aim is to

DOMINANT PERSONALITIES

There is no doubt that some foals have stronger, more aggressive personalities than others, but fortunately horse language is genetically programmed, so the cheeky foal already knows the signs which a dominant mare or stallion would use to say 'Shut up and behave yourself'! You can use this language too, and you may even have to frighten a really bossy foal into submission with dominant body language (see Stage 1) if he has no respect for humans; for instance you can squeal like a stallion or an annoyed mare, and kick out with the side of your foot or jab the foal with an elbow. This may seem a little unfair, but you will in fact probably only have to use aggressive tactics a couple of times before the foal realises he has overstepped the mark, and then you can continue imprint training as normal. In the wild he would soon be put in his place, but it is up to *you* to do this in a domestic situation, so that he doesn't develop into a difficult, rather stroppy horse which for the rest of his life will then invite abuse from the humans struggling to control him.

▲ You should only work for about fifteen minutes before giving the foal a break, for a maximum period of one hour in total the first day. Look for sucking motions of his lips which indicate that he needs to suckle

'programme' the foal's brain to accept your touch, and to teach him what you look, taste, sound and smell like. It is the unknown which will make a horse fearful, so by introducing yourself to the foal so early on and showing him that you mean no harm, you become a known quantity and he will never have cause to fear you.

It is important that you continue stroking after the foal relaxes under your touch, because he must show complete acceptance of what you are doing, not just tolerance. He already appreciates that you are highly significant to his life, although he doesn't know why, and he must also be persuaded that he has no option but to submit to you from the very start. Your presence there with his mother at the moment of his arrival into the world puts you in the role of friend or family, not predator, and he will soon realise that you are not going to hurt him; equally, he must also realise that it is always *you* who takes the initiative, not him.

There are no boundaries. Move along the foal's body, patting, stroking and squeezing him repeatedly until there is no area left untouched. Work all over his body, even between the back legs and underneath his tail, so that when the time comes for him to have his temperature taken or a tail bandage put on, the sensation will be familiar. Your touch should be confident and businesslike if you are to gain the foal's

complete confidence with the movement and pressure imitating the licking action of the mare.

When you have covered the foal's entire body, try to think of other sensations which he will need to become accustomed to as a domestic animal, even if it won't be for a few years. For example, you might run some clippers over his body and head (without actually taking any hair off!) so he gets used to the sound. Rustling pieces of paper and plastic bags all over and around him can also be part of the imprinting process, and anything else which will help to override that flight response and allay his fearfulness. And remember, you have to repeat each process at least thirty times for it to register permanently in a foal's subconscious mind.

The foal will remember all you have done at his birth even if you never repeat it again, but the process is obviously more effective if it is done regularly, perhaps for five minutes once a week after the initial imprinting. This is not always possible on large commercial studs, but for the home-bred youngster or small-time breeder it should be quite easy to fit in, and a pleasure.

WHAT IF I AM TOO LATE?

Mares can be very secretive about giving birth, but it is not a disaster if you miss the prime time for imprinting, immediately after birth. Imprinting is still possible several days later, although the longer you leave it, the more difficult it will be because the foal will have rapidly gained strength and confidence and you will no longer be the centre of his universe. Even so, you should still go through the whole imprinting process described above with a young horse of any age. It won't get any easier!

It is important that the youngster is not given the opportunity to use his strength against you if he is older and stronger, because undoubtedly he will then find out that he *can* get his own way. You will have to be much more determined and insistent, and it is advisable to halter-break him first (see Stage 3) both to establish a respectful relationship, and to give you a means of control before you attempt to overcome his fears by handling his vulnerable areas in the way described.

In spending time like this you are investing in your foal's future, and giving him a much better chance of becoming a good, reliable riding horse.

Do not get between the mare and her foal – it is vital that she bonds with her baby too, and they should always be nose to nose. This will reassure them both and make the imprinting easier for you. There are surprisingly few mares who resent the handler at this stage; if they do become aggressive or over-protective, this tends to happen a day or two later, in a herd situation. Of course, your relationship with the mare and her trust in you will dictate how tolerant she is towards your handling her foal so early on in his life.

Remember to work on both sides of the foal. Too few people realise the difficulty which horses have in translating what they have learned from one side to the other, and basically they will only learn from actual experience. If you were fully ambidextrous, just think of the advantages, because it's not just a question of which hand you write with, but your ability to co-ordinate and balance your body in everything you do. By handling both sides equally, you can lay the foundations for that sort of dexterity in your horse, and he will benefit for the rest of his life.

WORK WITH AN ASSISTANT

Once the foal has stood up and you are working over his body, it is a good idea to call in some help so that he does not slip away from you: have one person holding him and another imprinting. Foals can be strong and determined even so soon after birth, and if they do manage to wriggle out of your grasp, they will then unfortunately have learned that they are in fact physically stronger than a person and can use that strength to get their own way.

It is important not to grab the foal too hard, as if to prevent all movement, because this will probably have the opposite effect and cause him to struggle even more. It is also a way of antagonising him, besides which it pits your physical strength against the foal which is unfair, and is a battle you will ultimately lose. He must feel free to move, but when he realises that he is restricted, it should be in such a way as not to cause him to panic. Create a loose hold with your arm around his chest, and have the other arm ready to close in on his quarters and push them in the right direction.

It is good for the foal to be manipulated sideways, backwards and forwards in this way. Put an arm round his hindquarters and persuade him to execute mini 'turns on the forehand', so that he learns to swing his quarters away from pressure. Rather than pushing continuously, thus giving him something to lean against, touch and release as you would if you were giving an aid to a riding horse. This basic early lesson in moving away from pressure will prove invaluable when you come to halter-break, and later to back the young horse. Once he understands what you want, he will relax, and this may be the reason why studs which have used this technique in the USA have had consistently good results when breaking and training imprinted horses. They have found them to be easier and quicker to train, yet these horses haven't lost any of their competitive instinct; indeed, *because* they are relaxed, confident and well mannered, they are able to concentrate *all* their efforts into their performance.

As time goes on, the foal will grow more confident and will really enjoy the human contact. However, although he may come to see you as a friend to nip or nuzzle, too much of this behaviour is disrespectful, and he must *not* be allowed to carry on in this way. Flick his nose with a finger so as to discourage him, without frightening him; such behaviour may seem cute now, but when he is fully grown it could become a nasty habit. The message from you to him must be, 'We are friends, but I have the upper hand. I can touch you anywhere, in any place, at any time, but you can't touch me. Invading my personal space is by invitation only.'

OUT AND ABOUT

The final details of the imprinting process can be attended to when the foal is a little sturdier – for instance, by the time he is three days old, he can probably be loaded into a horsebox or trailer (because he is not yet halter-broken, he can follow his mother up and down the ramp); he might even be taken for a short journey, and indeed many foals travel early in life on their way to and from the stud.

Water is something else the foal must get used to. Trickling a hose or wet sponge up and down his legs is a good start and will not cause any harm, although avoid the head until he is more confident about the procedure; anyway, it is unlikely to cause a problem if he is used to being rubbed and handled all over his head already. However, do not wet his body unless it is a warm day. This is poor stable management with any horse, never mind a foal, and the principle behind all your training is to make sure that every experience is remembered as enjoyable. As you know yourself, a cool shower on a hot day is a different matter to a chilly hosing down in the middle of winter!

When the foal is halter-broken, he can join his

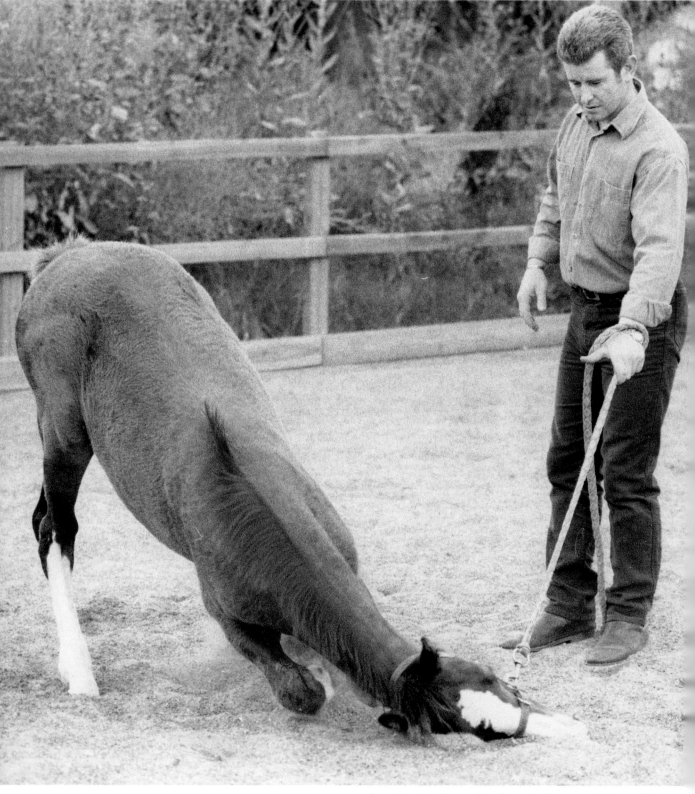

▲ Rather than having their feet picked up, some foals would rather lie down than submit! This is quite normal behaviour and is a way of evading the issue. Be persistent and stay calm

mother on rides and thus the imprinting process may be continued. You can lead him off the mare and introduce him to traffic around the yard, cross streams and ditches and see what he makes of other species of animal, such as goats and pigs.

HALTER-BREAKING AND TYING UP

The above lessons are not strictly part of the imprinting process, but the foal should learn them as soon as possible. Halter-breaking is a far more important experience for the horse than being just a convenient way of leading him to the field and back: it is the equivalent of teaching him the alphabet. It will be taken for granted in later years, but it forms the basis of the foal's whole education, and without it he cannot make progress or learn more complicated things. If he is halter-broken as described in the next stage, he will learn to give way to pressure, to respect you and your personal space, and to keep a careful eye on your body language, and this will effectively lay the foundations for his education as a riding horse.

STAGE 2
CHECKPOINTS

- ■ Imprint as early as possible; wiping off the new-born foal before he has got to his feet is a good start.
- ■ Stimulate every one of the foal's senses: touch, taste, smell, sight and hearing.
- ■ Work down both sides of the foal equally, because he will not transfer his knowledge from body parts on one side to those on the other.
- ■ Cover every inch and orifice of the foal's body.
- ■ Don't shut out the mare: she needs to bond with the foal too.
- ■ Allow mare and foal to stand nose to nose while you work over the foal, for their mutual reassurance.
- ■ Repeat the stimuli at least thirty times each, and continue even after the foal relaxes.
- ■ Work in fifteen-minute sessions, for a total of up to an hour on the first day.
- ■ Five minutes a week should be sufficient to refresh the foal's memory.
- ■ Work together – the foal must not get to know that if he struggles he can escape from you.
- ■ Go through the imprinting process as soon as you can with every young horse, even if you miss the optimum time after birth; however, it would be as well to halter-break him first.

STAGE 3
NURSERY

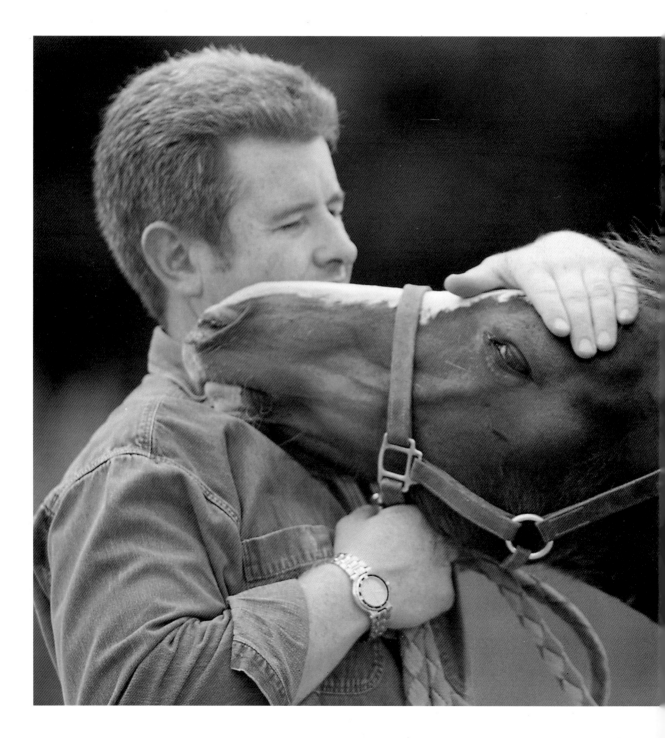

SCHOOL
Age: 6 weeks to 6 months

A foal is an example of a completely untrained, and in some cases untouched, flight animal. His life is dictated by pure instinct because he has no previous experiences, good or bad, to influence him. To the foal, the rules of life are simple but important: keep your distance from predators (which includes humans), stay with mother, and if in doubt, run! However, the foal's future is as a domestic animal, not a wild one, and leaving him to follow his natural instincts only makes his life more difficult.

If he is strong or stroppy many people will put off the halter-breaking process – they know it must be done some time, but they don't start as early as they should, especially when a foal is very young, because it often seems easier to leave his education until a later date. After all, he follows his mother everywhere you need him to go and causes no trouble – until you try and do things your way! But think of the people you know who have been riding, swimming or playing a musical instrument from such an early age that they don't even remember learning. They have no recollection of any difficulties experienced during early attempts, and their skill comes as second nature to them. You can achieve this with your foal, because good habits can become ingrained just as well as bad ones.

When the foal is about six weeks old, it is time to carry on where you left off after imprinting. A foal which has been imprinted has a head start, because the techniques which you use next will back up what you have already taught him. He has already submitted to you touching him all over, and now it must become second nature. A foal which has not been imprinted must start from square one.

The fact that foals vary in character must also be taken into consideration. Sometimes a foal will be bold and curious enough to approach you and find out for himself that you present no threat; others may be nervous and shy, and you will have to take extra trouble with these to win their confidence.

▲▼ While the young foal generally follows his mother closely enough not to need leading, he should still be handled individually on principle. While he will learn a great deal from his mother and will be reassured that she does not appear to find human beings frightening, he will not understand why she is so unperturbed: he must learn this for himself and it is your job to provide this experience

▲▼ Compared to other young mammals the foal is a sturdy and self-sufficient creature from the very start. He is strong enough to keep up with a galloping herd at just a few hours old, and he is also strong enough to put up a fight when you try some early handling such as putting on a headcollar or picking up his feet – your idea of domestic harmony is not the same as his at this stage, so you have to be determined, confident and persistent

ACCEPTING TOUCH

When you go to touch a foal it must be on your terms, and not on his. At every one of your short but frequent meetings, *you* must take the initiative and have the final word, though in the nicest possible way. In short, you are setting the precedent that when man is in the vicinity, what *he* wants is more important than anything that the horse might prefer to be doing. Moreover the idea that man requires instant respect and attention will hopefully endure throughout the rest of the horse's life and simplify every aspect of his future training.

Start with an area the foal does not mind having touched – a scratch along the neck and withers is usually popular as it imitates the way horses groom each other. Work your way around his body so that you are eventually touching more vulnerable areas such as the ribs, belly and between the front legs. Be careful not to tickle him – make every movement definite and significant with a firm pat or scratch. Lean right over the foal so that he feels your weight around his shoulders, then let go before clasping your arms around him again. Go to extremes and leave no area untouched: rub inside the ears and mouth, around the eyes and under the tail; then change sides and start all over again.

▲ Foals can appear friendly and inquisitive creatures at first, but very often they will only co-operate on their terms. As soon as they feel that *you* are taking control and imposing restraint on them, their fight/flight instinct takes over – basically they are only interested when it is *their* idea! As with any schooling process, don't even attempt to halter-break your youngster if you are not capable of seeing it through – and maybe collecting a few bruises on the way! Even so, the objections of a young foal or weanling are infinitely easier to handle than those of a 17hh horse which has been allowed to get away with things all his life

The areas you touch take on greater significance when you think of the saddle, girth, surcingle, bit, bridle, boots and bandages which one day the foal will wear; if he can tolerate you putting pressure on those areas now, his later training involving backing and being ridden will all come as much less of a shock to him. He may be curious about the smell or touch of the different pieces of equipment you will later introduce, but he should not actually fear them or panic when he feels them wrapped around him.

USING A STICK

When the foal is completely at ease with all this, and you can touch him all over without alarming him, take a short stick or jumping whip with a handkerchief tied to the end into the box with you. Allow the foal to

---

FACING FEAR

Handling is more for psychological, rather than physical reasons at this age, and the sooner the foal learns to face his fears – namely you, and all that you represent – and realises that he will survive the experience unscathed, the better for all concerned. The anticipation of fear is worse than the reality, so you will do your foal a big favour by tackling it for him sooner rather than later. Just a few hours' work over a period of weeks will help him to overcome his apprehension and hopefully eliminate the only major worry he has in his life: his fear of you, the predator. With quiet insistence and repetition you will break down his panic flight response, and this will stand him in good stead for the greater demands which will be made of him in later life, for instance when his training for being ridden begins. The 'fight or flight' response may be essential to keep the horse alive in the wild, but for the domestic animal, it keeps him in a state of unnecessary anxiety, and only serves to complicate his

investigate it, then instead of stroking with your hands all over his body, stroke him with your stick. He may be apprehensive at this new object, but he should have no cause to be frightened – and it is to be hoped that you are working with an animal which has never had reason to fear a raised stick in a human's hand. Once he has overcome all his anxiety at what you are doing, he should allow you to flap the handkerchief around his head and even drape it over his eyes.

If you are dealing with a foal or a young horse which has been abused, he will of course show fear at the sight of a stick or raised hand, and you will have to be particularly sympathetic; you may have to start with just a short stub of a stick without the handkerchief initially, and progress from there. Do not dismiss the exercise however; if anything, it is even more important for a previously abused horse to learn to tolerate this treatment so that eventually he is able to overcome his fear, and will recall the experience without alarm.

Natural Reactions

At any point the foal may leap sideways or kick out at what are very strange sensations for him, but you must persevere, and remember that this is nothing personal! As far as the foal is concerned, this pressure goes against his natural instinct, he feels sure that he should not allow it to happen, and he knows that you are the person responsible – he doesn't yet understand that you are a friend, and as far he knows, he's fighting for his life.

You must not punish the foal for reacting normally, but equally, don't allow *him* to control your reaction. Thus if *you* move away whenever he creates, you are in fact teaching him to associate making a fuss with causing the human to back off and stop making demands, and this is an idea which we want to keep out of his head at all costs: he must get used to yielding to pressure, and realise that it's up to him to find the comfort zone.

By 'restrained' I do not mean tied up or restricted in any way: the foal must be free to react normally, and then you can correct him, and in this way he learns that such behaviour won't get him anywhere. If you restrict his movement with sheer strength you will frighten him, and he is then hardly likely to feel any more confident in your presence. Moreover you will very soon not be *able* to control him physically, and then you will be in serious trouble.

Make life easier for yourself and for the foal by starting your handling in a relatively small, confined area such as a stable, and tie the mare up if she is likely to get in the way.

HANDLING THE MOTHER

The mare's temperament must always be considered when handling her foal, and she must be treated sympathetically and sensibly if she is nervous or very protective. The foal must not perceive this to be a traumatic experience in any way, and his mother's reaction will of course influence him. Thus if he sees her calmly munching hay, apparently unconcerned about what he perceives to be an attack on him, her baby, he will start to suspect that perhaps you are not life-threatening after all! Your behaviour must back up this suspicion, however, so it is imperative never to hurt the foal or demand anything unreasonable of him.

▲ The foal should respect the stick, but not fear it

▲ Watch the foal's expression and body language throughout and remember that his concentration span is very short. Look for signs of submission such as licking and chewing, or floppy ears. A tired and crotchety youngster won't learn much, so allow him to suckle and rest frequently. Schooling sessions need only last a few minutes provided that you finish anything you have started and end on a good note

ACCEPTING TOUCH

As you work over the head you are stimulating every one of the foal's five senses at once, and are cramming information about yourself into his subconscious. You need to touch him absolutely everywhere, and at least thirty repetitions of each stroke are needed for the lesson to register in his mind. He may be wary and suspicious initially as his flight instincts come to the fore, but the minor struggles he may put up at this stage are nothing compared to the stress he and you will suffer if you wait until he is a strapping weanling before beginning his education.

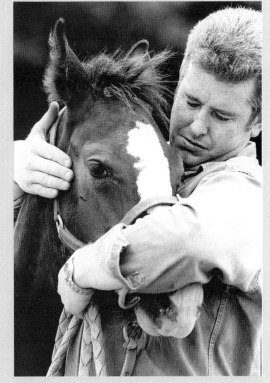

From the head, work down the neck to the chest, scratching and patting as you go. Run your hands over each leg, picking each one up gently and patting the bottom of each foot. The foal may try to move to his feet by now, and you must not prevent him doing this, nor should you stop him suckling when he wants to. Once he is standing, lean over him and encircle his body with your arms, squeezing the girth area gently. This may well provoke a strong reaction, but persevere until he submits and stands quietly. If you are tempted to give up, just consider the enormous favour you are doing this foal in preparing him for the girth, saddle and surcingle which will inevitably play such a huge part in his future life.

FEET FIRST

Think of all the things that you might ask of an adult horse, and incorporate suitable lessons into your early training of the foal. For example, it's never too early to teach him to pick up his feet — although this can be easier said than done! As an instinctively flight animal, the last thing your relatively untamed foal will want to do is deliberately 'disable' himself by standing on three legs, with the spare foot firmly in the hands of the enemy, because by doing so, he is giving up his best chance of survival if things go wrong. After all, in the wild a three-legged horse would undoubtedly be doomed.

So it is up to you to convince the foal that first, you are not the enemy, and that second, he can ignore his natural instincts and safely allow you to pick up his feet. Be assured that with patience and quiet insistence you will succeed in this. These photographs have been taken in the open for clarity but you should work in a loose box with the mare present. The foal should be loose so that he does not feel restricted or trapped; this is an exercise in trust between the two of you, and it is unfair to stack the odds in your favour — you will learn more about him if he is free to react. The more relaxed he becomes, the longer you will be able to hold his feet up, until eventually you will be able to pat the foot and put it down again when *you* choose. Moreover as the foal relaxes you should exert more control as to when the foot goes down, so that he gets out of the habit of snatching it away when *he* pleases.

Having his feet and limbs manipulated is a major hurdle, and once you have overcome it, the foal should be happy to let you handle the rest of his body. Now is your chance to poke your fingers gently into his ears, under his tail, even inside his mouth — this may seem a little excessive, but it will have the effect of making the youngster less touchy about being handled in these areas, and should make future events in his life such as being bridled or having his ears trimmed, less traumatic.

▲▼ You can see the unhandled foal's first reaction is to shy away from contact. Overcome this by working over his body, imitating the obviously pleasant mutual grooming actions you have witnessed between horses in the field: scratch along his crest, croup and withers, the top of his tail, under his belly and between his eyes

▲ As you get down to the foal's fetlocks, his natural reaction will be to pick his foot up and stamp it down to shake you off, as he would with an irritating fly. This is a natural reaction, and it is important to pat and reassure him. Don't try to hold the foot up at this point – it's not as easy as it appears for youngsters to balance on three legs, and he will understandably panic if he feels he's about to fall over

▲ The time between each stamp of the foot will become a little more prolonged at each attempt, until you can actually hold the foot up for a few seconds at a time. As the foal attempts to snatch it away, try to maintain contact with the leg throughout the process until he learns that while you present no threat, neither can you be shaken off

▶ Then move on to another foot – and be prepared to start all over again, because the foal will not necessarily transfer the lessons he has learned on one side of his body to the other, so don't be surprised if you are back to square one! Patiently repeat the process with every foot until the foal is comfortable, then get somebody else to try

▼ As time progresses, tap the feet with a hoofpick and extend the legs forwards and back as a farrier would do, until the foal is completely calm about this process

IN CASE OF DIFFICULTY...

If you have to deal with an unhandled foal, or an older horse which is reluctant to have his feet handled, there are other techniques which may help — and leaving the training until another day is not one of them! Teaching a youngster to allow his feet and legs to be handled is absolutely essential. Quite apart from the psychological advantage of him trusting you enough to pick up his feet, if the horse is used to feeling restrictions round his legs, then putting on boots or bandages should present fewer problems in the future, he will more readily become accustomed to the feeling of leg straps or long reins around his legs, and hopefully will not be unduly alarmed when shoes are fitted later in life. Moreover if accidents do occur, the horse will be less likely to panic and make

At this age, training is very basic, but the foal will still find it demanding mentally

very small foal! Next take your stick and handkerchief into the box and run it down each of the foal's legs. This will keep you out of range of any kick while he becomes accustomed to feeling things around his legs; even if he does kick out, you can persist until he realises that such behaviour does not make what is happening to him go away. When he behaves, you can reward him by removing the stick. He should be sufficiently confident with you and the stick not to be frightened and try to run away, yet the new sensation of the handkerchief tapping at his legs will almost certainly cause him to pick up the foot and stamp it down again, the first step in teaching him to pick his feet up. If he is determined not to pick up a foot, you may have to tap the leg quite firmly with your stick until you get a reaction. You know he can feel it, he is just ignoring you, so make yourself heard!

Using the stick keeps you out of harm's way initially, but you should work with your hands rather than the stick as soon as possible. If he picks his foot up slightly and stamps it down again, allow him to do so, but do not let go of the leg; if you do, you may be inadvertently training him to believe that such behaviour will effectively shake you off. At each attempt he should hold his foot in the air a little longer before trying to put it down, and it is important to take full advantage of the moments he does hold it up for you to praise and reassure him, making the experience of standing on three legs as pleasurable as possible.

The next stage is to teach the youngster to pick his foot up and put it down at your command, rather than just letting him make the decision when to do so. Tip one leg forwards so that it is resting on the toe; this is quite easy to do if you simply press on the back of the knee joint or allow the hock to flex naturally. The weight will be off the foot and, for a very brief moment, the foal should allow you to lift it off the ground. Do not try and lift it high — a couple of centimetres is plenty to start with, and you must give the foot back immediately, *before* the foal reaches the stage of wanting to snatch it back; then he has less opportunity to make a fuss, and you can praise him for good behaviour. Lifting the leg higher and for longer is just a matter of practice once you have established the basics. For a horse which seems 'frozen' to the ground, turn the head away to displace his bodyweight onto the other foreleg. Make allowance for the horse's lack of balance and do not try and hold the foot up for too long.

matters worse: for example he might get a foot stuck in wire in the field or out hacking — and while these things shouldn't happen, it is a fact of life that they do.

Begin by working as far down the top of each leg as you can from your 'hugging' position around the foal's neck. You should be able to reach a little way down the forearm and stifle on each side, although you won't get much further unless you are a very big person with a

HALTER-BREAKING

Most people realise how important it is to accustom their foals to a headcollar (also known as a foal slip) in the first few weeks of life. Physically and psychologically, wearing a halter and being led with a rope by a human are the foal's first lessons in discipline and obedience, and they mark a huge step towards its domestication. Unfortunately this vital early training is often badly done or is left incomplete, as is demonstrated by the alarming experiences that many people have with youngsters, or as a quick glance at youngstock classes in the show ring will illustrate. Just because your foal consents to having a halter on his head does *not* mean he is halter-broken, any more than a horse that allows a saddle to be placed on his back is fully broken for riding! Some of the most common problems I am asked to deal with in horses of any age, such as barging, napping, refusing to tie up or load into a horsebox, can be traced back to the fact that the horse was never properly halter-broken.

The good news is that you can start as soon as you like – it's never too early to have a polite foal that can be led independently of its mother. The earlier you start winning your foal's trust and handling him, the better, but be prepared to accept his limitations. Foals may appear to have plenty of energy, but they have a very short concentration span and will find their early lessons mentally exhausting, so a foal must be allowed to rest and suckle frequently.

Think of this stage of your horse's training as 'nursery school' – there is no place for long, complicated lessons or excessive discipline. Learning should be presented as a kind of game which is fun and rewarding to play.

A truly halter-broken horse is one that understands exactly what pressure means, not only responding instantly to the pressure on a headcollar, but beginning to anticipate it – by watching his handler's movements carefully he 'shadows' him/her so that the slack in the lead-rope remains constant at all times. The result is a horse that is a pleasure to handle, one that has

been 'tuned into' looking at and reacting to his handler's body language at a very early age.

Think of all the occasions when you need to handle the ridden horse's head on a regular basis. You need to put on a bridle and headcollar, check they fit correctly, wipe out the horse's eyes and ears when grooming, perhaps clip or trim around the head and pull the mane and forelock, fix a poll guard for travelling or a neck cover before he's turned out…the list goes on. Now think of all the horses you know which are headshy or difficult about any of the above procedures. There's usually at least one in every yard, and once physical discomfort such as poorly fitting tack or ear mites have

been eliminated, the reason is generally bad handling.

It goes against a horse's natural instincts to allow his head and other vulnerable areas to be handled, but if he is to be relaxed about the demands that will certainly be placed on him as a domestic horse, he must learn that you have the absolute right to touch him all over, even in his most vulnerable areas such as around his head or under his belly. There is a lot you can do to prepare your foal for life ahead, even when he is very young, so don't wait until you have a fully grown horse on your hands before trying.

Once he has truly understood this fundamental lesson, you have the beginnings of a trained horse; and when the time comes to put pressure on a bit in his mouth or a leg against his side, he should react by moving away from that, too.

INTO PRESSURE

It is important to understand that horses are 'into pressure' animals. An untrained horse will instinctively lean *into* a source of pressure, and teaching a horse to move away from pressure takes time and patience; this is one of the reasons why it takes years of schooling before you have an obedient, responsive ridden horse that reacts to subtle aids from the leg or hand. As you groom your horse, watch his reaction as you lean into him with each stroke of the body brush. What does he do? Lean right back of course, so that if you take the pressure away suddenly you can actually see him sway into the movement. Anyone who has ever leaned their shoulder or put a lunge line round the quarters of a horse that was reluctant to load will also have experienced 'into pressure', because the horse will sink back even further and virtually sit down in response to the pressure he can feel behind him.

Consider, too, the effect which this response will have on his ridden work: his instinct will dictate that if you pull him, he will pull you right back! So a heavy-handed rider is bound to make a hard-mouthed horse, and it's the same with work in hand.

When halter-breaking a foal, you must overcome this natural instinct to lean 'into pressure' by making it uncomfortable, and by rewarding him when he steps away from the pressure (see below). The method shown on pp42–3 works on any horse, from the foal to the bargy old horse that needs to be taught some manners in hand.

The foal must learn that pulling away from the rope makes life uncomfortable; whereas by bringing his head to you and allowing the rope to go slack, he enters the comfort zone

HALTER-BREAKING

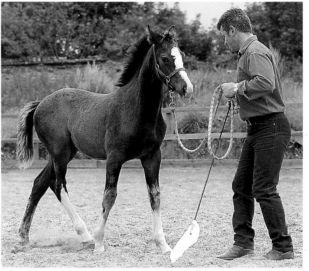

▲ Start with a well fitting halter and a long rope; with an older horse, try a 'controller' halter, or loop the rope over the top of his nose for your initial reschooling sessions. If your foal is very young, you must first teach him that he will be rewarded for keeping his head close to you. Start in the box carrying a short stick with a handkerchief attached to the end. Stroke the stick all over his body so that he is not afraid of it, then, holding the headcollar rope firmly, tap or tickle the foal's hindquarters with the stick and handkerchief until he moves them away from you

▲ This will naturally cause his head to swing round to you, at which point you must immediately release your hold on the rope and scratch the foal's forehead by way of reward. Repeat this process several times on each side until your foal begins to anticipate the action of the stick and swings his head towards you before you even make contact with his quarters. His reward for this action *must always* be a pat and an *immediate* release of the pressure on his headcollar, and a cessation of the irritation of the stick on his quarters. *Never* hit the horse with the stick: the aim is not to cause fear or pain but to initiate a logical learning process. This foal has felt the pressure increase and knows where he has to go to relieve it

TEACHER TRAINING

A common mistake is to hold the rope too short, so that the hand is right under the horse's chin, the handler trying to hang on and direct movement. According to the 'into pressure' principle previously explained, this will only encourage the horse to pull against you and to barge, whereas you are working on prevention rather than cure. You wouldn't smack an innocent child just in case it *planned* to do something wrong – you would wait until it had actually made a mistake, because then you can turn the situation to your advantage and school him: thus if you allow plenty of slack, the horse is free to make a mistake and you are free to

▲ Once your horse is happy with this, you can start to take him out for walks. Walk level with his shoulder or slightly in front of it, and if he tries to pull past you, dig your heels in so that he is brought to a short, sharp halt. Bring his head round to you, allow the rope to slacken, and then reward him with a pat or scratch. The message must be clearly, 'Here is the comfort zone. Stick with me and you'll be all right – do your own thing and you will make life uncomfortable.' Continue to carry your stick and handkerchief if necessary so that you can reinforce the message. With a foal, make sure that it really is *you* dictating the pace, and that he is not just following his mother. If a foal is properly halter-broken it should be possible to walk him away from his mother and even out of sight for very short distances

correct it, whereas if you stifle the horse's initiative and try to prevent every false move, he will learn nothing. It is for him to watch and shadow your movements, not the other way round.

When you are sure that the horse has understood the lesson (probably after several days), you can put your halter-breaking to the test by making sharp turns or changes of pace as you lead the horse in hand; he should follow you without the rope becoming taut, taking great care to keep his head close to you in the 'comfort zone'. If his attention wanders, pick up the stick and tap his quarters away from you or take a short, sharp jerk and release on the headcollar to remind him which is most comfortable.

Problem Solver
THE BARGY HORSE

The truly halter-broken horse is very conscious of the area of personal space surrounding the handler (see Stage 1) and is careful not to intrude into it, so you are highly unlikely to suffer squashed toes or be knocked over if the horse shies. Halter-breaking reinforces the message of personal space, and a good exercise for a horse that is inclined to be strong or to push people around is to make him back up in hand. Adopt your aggressive stance (see Stage 1) and approach the horse head on. If he doesn't back off in response, flick or rattle the lead-rope at him until he takes a step back, then stop and reward him. You are asserting your authority absolutely, and reminding him that you are in charge. The horse must also learn that the issue of 'personal space' is something of a one-way thing: it is always acceptable for you to enter his personal space and touch him whenever you like, but he must wait to be invited into yours. It's a matter of keeping his respect, and ensuring that *you* still hold the casting vote should there be any disagreements between the two of you.

▶ A horse which is properly halter-broken and respects your personal space should back up in hand without any fuss

▼ You may have to be a little harder on the bargy horse which needs reschooling, and even resort to using a controller halter or a rope across the top of his nose to get him to respect pressure. As he walks past your shoulder and begins to take control of the situation, dig in your heels and make him turn towards you

FIGURE OF EIGHT

If the foal is very unruly and has started to pit his strength against you, try leading him in a 'figure of eight'. This is a rope, a piece of webbing or a soft bandage which passes around his quarters, knots at the withers and runs down the shoulders and over the chest. It gives the handler greater control and encourages the foal to move forwards or backwards, depending on where the pressure is applied. If the foal does kick out or object in any way, it will not come off, unlike the traditional technique of putting a stable rubber around the foal's quarters. The foal should wear his headcollar and lead rope as normal, and the figure of eight should only be used to back up your commands when necessary.

STAGE 3
CHECKPOINTS

- Keep sessions short and sweet.

- Teach the foal to lead properly as soon as possible – correct halter-breaking will influence all his future training.

- Picking up a foal's feet is not just a good preparation for the farrier's visits; it indicates that he has put his trust in you, and this is a significant decision for a flight animal to make.

- Don't avoid confrontation if it is really necessary: the foal grows stronger by the day, and it is your responsibility to stop him turning into a problem horse.

- Take the foal's character into consideration when handling him: some are naturally bolder than others.

- Do all preliminary training sooner rather than later, the foal's learning curve is steepest immediately after birth.

- Now is the time to handle vulnerable areas, and don't let the foal 'train' you to avoid touching them.

- Think of the equipment that the foal will one day wear and base your handling around 'desensitising' the relevant areas of his body.

- Remember that you are setting a precedent for the rest of the foal's life, and his future attitude to humans depends on how you handle him.

TEENAGE

REBELLIONS
Age: 6–18 months

No matter how well you try to bring up your 'child', there invariably comes a time when he will decide to test you out and become rebellious. With horses, this is usually when they would be mature enough to leave the wild herd or to start to breed, when they are technically 'teenagers'. Their instinct and hormones tell them to assert themselves in the name of survival, and physically they are indeed adult; however, they have none of the calm confidence and experience of the older, wiser horse.

In domestic horses the rebellious streak may surface at any time, and it often does so when a new owner or handler takes over. I can honestly say that it is not in a horse's nature to be deliberately nasty, so we may assume that all he is trying to do at this stage is find out if you are a worthy leader. You can't blame him for this, since he comes from a world where a strong leader is essential to safeguard the survival of the herd. The important thing is that when he asks the question, *you* are able to convince him as to why you *should* be the boss, and ignoring the question will only cause him to keep on challenging your authority. Your behaviour must therefore command his respect by being firm, fair and reasonable. This doesn't mean you have to be hard on him, but never seek to ingratiate yourself with him by lenient handling. A horse will not like you any more for being soft and letting him get away with bad manners; on the contrary, he is far more comfortable when he can respect you. Think back to your favourite teacher at school, the one for whom you always did your homework on time; it was probably neither the 'nicest' teacher, nor the one you feared most, but the one you both liked and respected – and if you fully understood the subject they taught, so much the better!

In the horse's wild state it is the dominant mares which are responsible for keeping the peace and instilling good manners when the teenagers start to find their feet. In their absence, the human handler must take on the role of teacher and disciplinarian, because if bolshy behaviour is allowed to go unchecked, the domestic horse is unlikely to grow out of it. You may have a good understanding of what you are trying to establish and your horse may be capable of achieving it, unless you insist on working it out, but your relationship will still lack the essential ingredient for success: respect.

JOIN-UP

In recent years, as Monty Roberts' methods and my own have become better known, people have become very excited about the concept of 'join-up'. Join-up is a perfectly simple process which makes use of the horse's natural instincts to flee in response to a perceived threat. *You* are that perceived threat, because the horse sees you as a predator, for the reasons already discussed in Stage 1. An understanding between the predator and the preyed upon can only be to the latter's advantage, however, and the horse knows it, although it may take time to allay his suspicions altogether and to make him realise that your offer to be his friend is absolutely genuine. Once he has accepted this, his equivalent of 'shaking hands' on the deal is to join up with you. The horse is an honest and generous business partner, and as far as he is concerned, once he has given his word and joined up, his decision is virtually irreversible.

Once you have reached an agreement and achieved join-up, this generous attitude of the horse means he is usually only too pleased to oblige whenever he can, provided he feels he can trust you. This puts you in a very strong position as regards asking for favours – such as, how about we put on this saddle and you let me sit on your back? This is why join-up makes it possible (although not necessarily desirable) to back an unhandled horse in under thirty minutes, as Monty Roberts has demonstrated several times. He uses join-up and the psychology of trust, rather than the traditional method of lengthy repetition, to teach a horse to accept tack and a rider.

Although equine psychology and an understanding of body language are necessary, join-up is essentially a physical process; moreover every horse will respond, and every observant handler can achieve it. A horse does not have to be wild to respond, although the less handled the horse, the more blatant its demonstration of instinctive behaviour will be. Even the oldest, most domesticated horse still remains enough in touch with its primitive instincts to respond to join-up tactics until the end of its days, so it is never too late!

STARTING TO JOIN UP

Join-up is also known as 'advance and retreat' because it involves putting psychological pressure on the horse by driving him away from you, then backing off and giving him the chance to seek your company, the comfort of which is his reward; this he is normally eager to do, rather than allow you to put the pressure on him again.

It is best to start in a small enclosed space such as a stable. It has been proved that join-up can be achieved with a wild mustang on the open ranges, but for ease and practicality it is wise to give the horse a little less freedom while you try and get the message across! He will have been given his first notion about

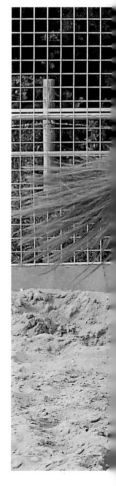

▶ A horse which is completely unrestrained but which shadows a human's every move, following in his footsteps like a dog, seems to indicate the sort of mystical communion enjoyed by so-called 'horse whisperers'. Many people regard it with wonder, and seem to believe it signifies a rare and perfect understanding between horse and handler, accessible only to those with a special gift. Fortunately for us all, this is completely untrue

---

GAINING HIS RESPECT

Size isn't everything, and in fact when it comes to handling horses, size isn't anything because even the smallest horse is stronger than the biggest human; so there is no point in making any aspect of the horse's training a battle of strength, as you will certainly lose. Yet the people whom I seem to see most often struggling with problems of disrespect, barging and aggression are small women with large Warmblood-type horses. Sometimes these horses are fine with other people in the yard, and only use 'power play' against their diminutive owners – ironically, the very ones who are trying their hardest to gain pleasure and enjoyment from their horses.

These cases highlight the importance of using mental rather than physical tactics in the management of horses, and bring us back to the fundamental lessons which a foal should learn from the start: acceptance of your presence and authority, correct halter-breaking and a respect for your personal space. Whatever the problem, the solution – or at least the beginning of it – lies in re-establishing these basics.

join-up from his initial halter-breaking (see Stage 3), so you must start with this stage if you have not already done so. Halter-breaking puts the clear idea into the horse's mind that to be with you is pleasant, and to oppose you is not – and full join-up is a logical progression from this.

Put a headcollar and rope on the horse and carry a stick in your other hand. Stand alongside the horse and position yourself so that each arm makes two sides of the triangle, as if you were going to lunge him on a lead-rope in a tiny circle around his box. Stroke the stick gently on his quarters until he moves them away from you, and at the same time, exert gentle pressure on the headcollar to get him to bring his head into you. If he is slow to respond, tap his quarters harder with the stick until you are using the minimum level of force necessary to make him move round. Some horses may kick out at the stick initially, particularly young ones which are not used to having things around their back end, so do not stand where you might be within reach.

If the horse makes just one step in the right direction this is sufficient to start with, and it is vital that you loosen your hold on the headcollar rope immediately and rub the horse between the eyes to reward him for bringing his head to you. In fact his reward will be two-fold, because as his head swings round towards you, his quarters naturally swing away, so as well as receiving a scratch, the irritation of the stick touching his quarters will cease. It will not take him long to work out what he has to do in order to gain this double reward, and he will begin to anticipate your movements and swing his head round of his own accord. When this happens, remove the headcollar and see if he will keep swinging his head to you without any physical encouragement. When the horse does come to you, it is a sign of both physical and psychological submission – so make him bring his head down to chest height and present himself properly for his reward, rather than you having to stretch up to reach his head.

Once the horse has reached the stage where he is reading your body language and no longer waits for you to touch him with the stick or pull on the lead-rope, you can turn him loose in a larger area to take what he has just learned a step further.

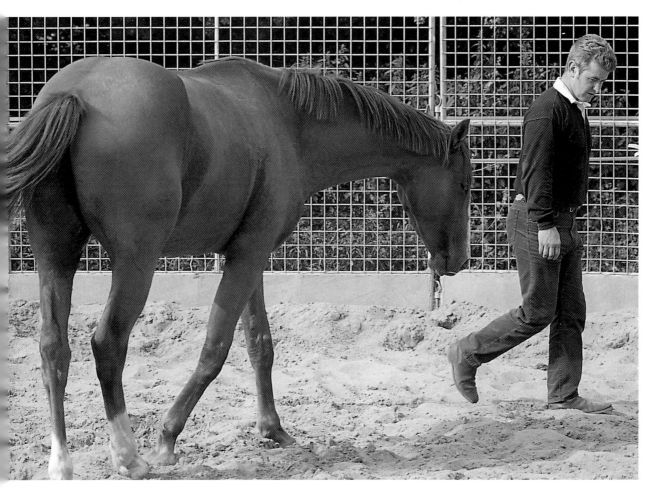

THE VITAL SIGNS

A young horse in the pen for the first time – his inside ear locks onto the person in the centre and acknowledges their importance in his life

The horse stops and thinks about the situation. He doesn't want to run any more, but he's not sure what to do next

Licking, chewing and direct eye contact. This horse is ready to come to the negotiating table and talk business

WORKING IN THE PEN

The success of working your horse in a pen or confined area is based on his strong herd instinct. The horse likes company of any kind: he feels threatened and vulnerable outside the social group, and associates being sent away from the herd as a punishment – this would probably be inflicted on him by the dominant stallion or mare in his group. Bear this in mind as you stand in the middle of the schooling area and 'chase' the horse away from you using aggressive body language. His natural reaction will be to go to the limits of the confined space and trot around you, and he must learn to perceive the outer ring of the pen as a 'bad' place to be, because it is the place where he is completely alone and therefore insecure, and the centre of the circle, with you, he must come to consider as a 'good' place to be.

As he trots or canters round look carefully for signs of submission – softening around the muzzle, licking and chewing, lowering the head and turning an ear or even the eyes towards you. He is saying 'OK, I give in – I want to be with you and I'm ready to talk.' It is important that you note these signs and reward them: they are your cue to ease up on the horse and give him the chance to take the favourable option, which is to return to you. If you miss the signs of submission and continue to press the horse with aggressive body language, you are effectively saying 'Stuff your apology, I'm not interested in negotiating,' and this will confuse and demoralise him. Soften your body language, adopt a more passive stance, and see if the horse shows signs of coming to you. There must be no half-hearted agreements here – he must come right up to you for his reward. If he loses interest or becomes hesitant, send him away again aggressively until he makes up his mind. The process usually has to be repeated several times, and much more often with a horse which has lost faith in humans through bad or inconsistent handling.

The sole reward for the horse's submission is your company, touch and praise: there must be no food or bribe involved, because this gives the horse an ulterior motive for coming to you. Reward him for coming with a scratch or pat; a nervous horse may well fly back to the outer edge of the circle and begin to canter round again, but this is fine, because he is free to act as he pleases – however, by doing so he has chosen to put himself back on the lonely outer edge of the circle. Next time you will find that he will not run off quite so far or so fast!

PUTTING JOIN-UP TO THE TEST

The horse is now physically and mentally under pressure – physically because you are sending him on and making him work, and mentally because he dislikes being out on his own at the edge of the circle. There is nothing that makes a herd animal feel more uncomfortable than to be isolated; remember how in the wild, the dominant mares will use this method to frighten youngsters into behaving themselves, sending them away from the rest of the group like naughty children who are sent to their room to consider their bad behaviour! It is only when they have apologised and seen the error of their ways that they are allowed back into the safety and comfort of the herd.

As a result of your early training with the stick and halter, your horse already sees you as this 'comfort zone', and will soon show signs of wanting to be 'allowed back in' – in this case, back to you at the centre of the circle. To miss or ignore such signs is to throw his apology back in his face, and to do so may damage your relationship.

▲ Ideally I use a round pen of twenty metres in diameter, but if you can fence off a similar-sized corner of a school or field with bales or poles, this will do just as well

▲ Stand in the middle with a lunge whip or long rope which you can flick at the horse's back end to send him away from you. You have no hold on his head any more, and his natural reaction will be to take off around the perimeter of the schooling area at a brisk trot or canter

▶ For a start he will think that being able to indulge his natural flight reflex in this way is fine, but as you continue to send him on he will realise that it's no fun when it's not his idea! He may be loose, but you are still controlling the situation and dictating his actions. Try using your body language to turn the horse by running forwards to cut off his route, then send him away in the other direction

VULNERABLE AREAS

You are turning the horse's world upside down by suggesting that predator and flight animal can be friends and 'join up', so never underestimate the enormity of what you are asking; at the back of his mind will probably still lurk the suspicion that there are risks involved. To interact with a predator goes against all his natural instincts and his better judgement — it must seem rather like accepting a dinner invitation to the lion's den! Ironically, the next step involves asking him to put his head between your jaws, as it were, the equine equivalent being for the horse to allow the predator access to his vulnerable areas: his belly, over his neck, around his head and ultimately his legs and feet. A horse on three legs in the presence of a predator is as good as dead, and he knows it, so it is the ultimate act of trust on his part. Once the horse has approached you and 'joined up', leave him loose and work over his body with your hands until he is happy to let you touch him anywhere you please.

Touching the horse softly and quietly in those areas where a predator would normally choose to attack is the best way to allay his final fears and suspicions, and in time and through experience he will learn that you won't betray him. It is only when he has put his life on the line in this way and realised that he comes back unscathed, that the horse will breathe his final sigh of relief and trust you completely.

SUBMISSION

When the horse is showing signs of submission clearly and frequently, give him the opportunity to come back to you if he wants to. Stop driving him away and stand still. Encourage him with submissive body language (see Stage 1), although do not walk forwards to meet him halfway — he must come right up to you to show complete submission. If he loses interest halfway across the arena, or hesitates or wanders off, then send him away again to the outer edge of the schooling area with aggressive body language. He must make up his own mind which situation he finds most comfortable, and logically, it will be you in the end.

When the horse has come right up to you and stands with his head lowered towards you in the middle of the arena, reward him with your touch and praise — but no titbits. It is essential that he joins up with you for the right reasons — namely, because he likes and respects you, and wants to be in your company, *not* because he has been bribed.

From this point on it is just a matter of strengthening the bond and building on what the horse has learned. When his interest and desire to be with you wanes, send him away to the outer edge of the schooling area again — in this way you are telling him that if he wants to be on his own that's fine by you, he's free to go, but he will do it on *your* terms, so he must go right away and work on his own. This will remind him of what his alternatives are, and should strengthen his resolve to stay a little closer to you next time!

Each time he should be more reluctant to make the mistake which results in him being sent away to work on his own, and will follow you more closely. Once he has had a chance to weigh up the alternatives he will invariably decide to take the easy, most comfortable option, which is of course to be with you. If the horse is very fit or nervous then he will not need or want to give in too soon — but however long it takes, *you* must remain the comfort zone: for successful join-up, the horse must believe implicitly that every time he comes to you, he will find comfort, without fail.

▶ See how much attention he is now paying to your body language. If you move or walk away, does he watch and make a move to follow you? He is unlikely to stick to you very closely at this stage, but he might well take a few tentative steps which you can reward

▲ Watch carefully for signs such as licking and chewing, lowering of the head and neck, or an ear or eye locking on to you, or the horse may even actually stop and turn in to you

▲ The horse will be ready to submit more quickly each time you send him away, so as soon as you see the signs, assume a passive posture to show him that you don't bear grudges and that he is free to return to you for his reward again

As your join-up technique becomes more subtle, you should not even have to send the horse away when his attention drifts from you – a sharp movement will regain his concentration and remind him that while you are in his presence, *you* take precedence over all other things in his life.

USING JOIN-UP

Join-up comes into its own with a difficult horse or an adolescent testing your authority. It is obvious how it will help a horse which is difficult to catch – from that point on you won't be able to get rid of him! But familiarity can breed contempt, and as the horse grows in confidence and strength he may feel that the balance of your relationship is swinging in his favour. He may stop seeing you as quite so much of a predator and more as he would another horse, whose authority is there to be challenged. This is when handling problems can start to arise, and when the horse's memory of the natural order of things needs refreshing. Use a round pen or other enclosed area to re-establish join-up and so make it quite clear who is the predator and who the flight animal. No matter how many bad manners a horse has developed, he will never forget his natural instincts completely until the day he dies. Whilst it becomes less and less likely that the safest old pony in the world will shy or buck, for example, it is always possible. Those instincts will always lurk somewhere below the surface, and you use this certainty to your advantage when establishing join-up.

Join-up allows you to discipline the horse without ever raising a hand: you will never need to hit him or to pit your strength against him, because your relationship transcends the physical. You have placed yourself at the top of the herd hierarchy and the horse has found out for himself that it is in his best interests to be nice to you; having tried the alternatives, he has discovered that the best place for him to be is with you, even though you will only permit him to enjoy your company if he behaves. He knows that you are the stronger of the two, but that you will be fair if he plays by the rules – to a joined-up horse, being out of your favour is enough to worry him and make him appear remorseful for his rude behaviour, since thousands of years of evolution have instilled in his mind that a single horse is doomed.

As a natural consequence of join-up the horse is highly tuned to your body language and gestures, and respects both you and the space around you. When he is in your presence he will not want to do anything

which may jeopardise your friendship, and this makes him very keen to please and easy to handle. The effect is particularly noticeable in previously bargy or aggressive horses. Note, too, that when a horse is 'joined-up' he must always follow just behind you – and it should never be the other way around. You will always be the predator, albeit a friendly one, and the horse must accept without compunction that you still take the initiative. Remember that this is a partnership, but not a completely equal one in that you still have the casting vote.

ALLOW FOR CORRECTION

It is easy to become defensive, and to try to anticipate and prevent any misbehaviour, but it is actually better to allow the horse to make mistakes so that you have the opportunity of correcting them. You wouldn't smack an innocent child just *in case* it planned to do something wrong – you would wait until that child had actually *made* a mistake, and would then react accordingly. Barging or pulling when being led is a good example of this: by holding on tight to the lead-rope to try and prevent the problem, you actually *cause* it by giving the horse something to barge against.

Instead, you should invite the horse to misbehave

▲ If the horse goes past you when being led in hand, let him go, but then dig in your heels and jerk his head sharply towards you, as you would a dog which pulled on its lead

so that you can turn the situation to your advantage and school it; therefore allow plenty of slack so the horse is free to make a mistake, and you can then correct it. If you stifle the horse's every movement and try to prevent any false move he might be at risk of making, he will learn nothing. It is for him to watch and shadow your movements, not the other way round.

A bridle is often used to give added control, but it will damage the horse's mouth if you have to school him for bad behaviour. In any case, the object of the exercise is to teach the horse to respect the pressure of a halter, and not to find a stronger alternative — you can't tie a horse by its bridle to the side of your lorry at a busy show! Once he has learned his lesson it won't matter whether it is a human or a tie-ring at the other end of the rope; he will always relent to the pressure.

Imagine trying to load a difficult horse: he may not like the look of the lorry, but to him it will no longer be an option to pull against the pressure of the headcollar and he will have to follow you in.

▲ If the bargy individual is slightly older, I clip a rope or chain on one side of the headcollar and pass it over the horse's nose and through the ring on the other side. This gives a 'choke chain' effect, and it can be rattled against the horse's nose to deter him from leaning into it and pulling

MENTAL EXERCISE

A horse under the age of three years old is not physically strong enough to carry a rider for any sort of distance without causing damage to itself, and the equine skeleton is not fully mature until the age of six. However, mental exercise is a completely different matter. Some horses, particularly the more clever and talented ones, become bored quickly, and like children in search of fun, can end up looking for trouble in the absence of any other form of stimulation.

Forget the textbooks for a while and use your own judgement and knowledge of your horse's character to decide whether he is ready to learn more, or whether he actually needs more time off to assimilate the lessons he's learned so far. In this, every horse is an individual; for instance, I have found that entire colts in particular can be precocious, and may need their energy directing in a constructive way, as any naughty youngster. Thus while the immature horse cannot carry the weight of a human, he can learn about equipment and be taught how to wear it long before he is actually backed.

Provided that he is properly halter-broken you will be safe to introduce him to hazards he will eventually encounter out hacking, such as cars, dogs and cyclists. As regards management it is always a joy to deal with a horse which will stand still to be hosed or to have fly repellent applied, or when his rugs are straightened or a wormer is given — so work on this now. You should also be sure that the youngster spends sufficient time in the field playing rough games with other youngsters, working off all his pent-up energy and aggressions; then after play time it may be quite reasonable to expect him to come back to the 'classroom' refreshed and ready to start again.

FINAL NOTES

A well mannered animal has an easier life and so does his handler, but your horse is what *you* make it. In fact he is not the only one with lessons to learn — you have, too! Be guided by his reactions, and always be fair and consistent in your handling; all discipline needs to be appropriate and effective. With youngsters particularly, it should be enough to make them sit up and pay attention, without causing pain or fear.

There must be no doubt in your mind that the horse understands exactly what you are asking of him, and is both physically and mentally capable of doing it for you. If you are not completely sure of this, then you won't know whether he needs discipline or encouragement, if he is being naughty or is genuinely frightened. To punish a horse without reason is unforgivable and it will make him bitter and unco-operative very quickly indeed if you get it wrong.

The important thing is not to panic or to back off should your horse start to test your authority. Every time he becomes cheeky or throws a teenage temper tantrum, look on it as an opportunity to strengthen and develop your relationship with him; this will help you to keep a positive outlook and will therefore give you a greater chance of success. Well handled, minor behavioural problems will actually help you to gain his respect more, not to lose it.

Equine teenagers must be handled tactfully, but nonetheless should be made to realise that rudeness is absolutely not an option. They can test you by all means – it is bold and intelligent of them to do so – but they should come up against the same consistent reaction and the same answer, every time they try: 'no' always means 'no', not 'maybe'!

It must all be black and white to the horse at this stage. I have seen alarming examples of what happens when a horse strays unchecked into a grey area – for instance an irritating habit can quickly turn into a full-blown and dangerous behavioural problem, to the extent that the owner considers putting the horse down. Prevention is so much easier than cure when handling a young horse.

STAGE 4
CHECKPOINTS

- Be sure that the horse is mentally and physically capable of doing as you ask.

- Don't worry unduly or overreact if you run into a problem – it is normal for an intelligent horse to test you out.

- Remember the herd hierarchy system: are you proving to be a fair and worthy leader?

- Never try and avoid problems or put them off until another day. The horse needs a definite and satisfactory answer to his questions the moment he asks them.

- Don't try and ingratiate yourself with a horse by sentimental or excessively lenient handling. He won't respect you for it.

- Never reduce an argument to a trial of strength: use mental tactics and body language.

- Always reward the positive rather than punish the negative.

- At the first sign of a problem, re-establish the basics: halter-breaking and join-up reinforce your superior position, they teach respect for your personal space, and remind the horse that you are the comfort zone.

- Don't anticipate or try to prevent bad behaviour. Go out of your way to set up a situation where it *will* happen, then you can take the opportunity to school the horse's mistake.

- Allow no grey areas to creep into your relationship. Black and white will give the horse confidence.

STAGE 5
HANDLING THE ENTIRE
All ages

Entires have many qualities. They are generally intelligent, full of character, bold and assertive; they are also well muscled and physically strong. When the stallion is well managed, and his behaviour properly understood and respected, these qualities can be used to the rider's advantage: put his superior strength and intelligence to the test in top class competition, and you could have a world-beater, as many professional horsemen and competitors will testify. For the quality animal that has a good temperament as well as real ability and performance, potential stud fees add to the attraction.

The entire's temperament depends to a great extent on the manners he is taught as a youngster and the handling he receives thereafter. He must be handled firmly but with sensitivity, making allowances for his natural instincts but without compromising on good behaviour; it's a fine line which calls for judgement and experience. Moreover stallions won't be intimidated by bullying because they're intelligent enough to know that a bully is weak beneath the bluster, and even when you have earned an entire's respect, his natural libido to be the best and the strongest means that he is bound to keep testing you out. As far as he is concerned, it only makes good sense to keep checking that the professed leader of the herd is up to the job – in his natural world, where only the fittest and brightest survive, lives depend on it. Therefore examine your motives for having a stallion: he is not a prize, and there is much more involved than simply exerting your mastery over him. If you are doing it for the wrong reasons, then you will undoubtedly run into trouble.

When an entire decides to test the capabilities of his rider or his handler, an experienced professional should be confident and competent enough to rise to the challenge; however, it can be different for the ordinary rider. If a stallion takes advantage of the situation, then half a ton of plunging horseflesh can be very intimidating! Having said this, although entires are generally unsuitable for a less experienced person, they are often a real pleasure to ride; problems usually begin much earlier, at ground level, because of poor handling and stable management.

LONG-TERM OBJECTIVES

Stallions need to be well mannered enough to be seen out and about, to prove that they have both the temperament and ability to make them worthy sires. The ultimate aim with any stallion should be to integrate him as well as possible with the rest of the yard, for his own health and happiness; far from making him territorial and difficult, this will actually make the handler's job much easier because he will then be dealing with a relaxed and happy horse. Once the ground rules have been set, and the stallion shows himself to be a well disciplined individual, in the hands of a competent rider there is no reason why he should not be lunged, schooled, travelled and hacked out with other horses. He can even be turned out near them, although obviously not in the same paddock. He simply needs to be taught that there is more to life than covering mares, and a clear line should be drawn between his stud duties and ridden work.

There is a close association between the way a stallion behaves in hand and the way he reacts under saddle. If a stallion is competing at a show, the rider should not be screaming at everyone and warning them to keep their distance 'because he's a stallion'. Even in these circumstances, it should make no difference because the horse should know that he is there to do a different job, and be disciplined enough to get on with it. In order to get this message across, use different equipment for stud duties and ridden work, and maintain as regular a routine as possible. For example, keep one bridle for covering and a different one for riding. Never try and school the stallion in the area where he normally covers mares, and keep him to a strict daily timetable — for instance,

▼ The fact that a horse is entire shouldn't make any difference to his training, because good handling and discipline do not rely on physical strength – thus a bad-mannered Shetland gelding can make life much more miserable than a well handled Thoroughbred stallion! From day one there must be no compromises and no concessions whatsoever in the stallion's training. Moreover it is vital that he is properly halter-broken and that he respects your personal space, as explained in Stages 1 and 3

▲ It is important that a stallion is properly halter-broken, as explained in Stage 3. To ensure that you have complete control at all times it may be necessary to pass a chain from the lead-rope, through the side ring of the headcollar and across the horse's nose. The effect of this is rather like a dog's choke chain – the 'zipping' action and the rattling of the chain against the bone of the horse's nose make a noise that catches his attention and also causes mild discomfort if he pulls against it. The benefit of leading a horse with a headcollar and chain rather than a bridle is that should any disagreements arise, you can school him without damaging his mouth

ride in the morning, and cover mares in the afternoon. In this respect you must be highly disciplined with yourself because the horse must understand exactly where his boundaries are – if you handle him inconsistently you will confuse him, and this will cause trouble for you. Given an inch, the stallion will always take a mile.

When a stallion is well managed, it often happens that he actually begins to discipline himself when others do not: for instance, presented with a new handler or a potential weak link, he may think about behaving badly, but then good habits override his boisterous impulses and he can be seen to check himself; thus the handler no longer has to keep reminding him who is boss every step of the way.

▲ When leading a stallion, stand to one side and make sure that you always lead him with a sufficiently long piece of rope so you can keep hold without being 'sucked under' the horse if he does rear. Pulling him to one side can unbalance him sufficiently to bring him down off his hind legs, but if rearing becomes a real problem you must take steps to cure it before it gets out of hand. Halter-breaking with a chain over the stallion's nose, as pictured, is the first step. He must learn to respect both you, and your personal space again, and realise that this is about tactics, not physical strength

Respect your stallion, but don't be in awe of him. If he is well brought up there is no reason at all why he can't be polite and manageable when kept alongside other horses. Stallions are certainly selective creatures and soon recognise who is a soft touch, but they also need to be versatile. It's no good if only one person can handle the horse, because sooner or later someone else will need to take over, for one of a hundred different reasons. If this isn't possible, then you cannot claim that your stallion is well behaved.

STABLE MANAGEMENT

The day-to-day management of any stallion must be considered carefully: problems frequently arise because they are subjected to an unnatural stable management routine. While it can be impractical to keep a stallion in an ordinary yard where other horses and riders roam free, this is not *his* fault, and if you want him to behave like a normal horse – apart from the fact that he can cover mares – then you must treat him like one.

All too often stallions are stabled away from the rest of the yard, are rarely turned out, and are even exercised separately. This is enough to make even a gelding with the mildest of manners horribly grouchy, never mind a hot-blooded male who is constantly on the lookout for excitement and entertainment! Any horse (or human!) who feels bored, frustrated and unhappy will be tricky to handle. The horse is a herd animal and keeping a stallion isolated is cruel, however well fed and carefully looked after he may be.

▲ I have had stallions resident in my yard on several occasions, some with behavioural problems caused entirely by bad management; all of them have been kept alongside others, in stables where they can touch and smell their next-door neighbour. Life is generally quite noisy for a day or two, then things settle down – and within a week, visitors are astonished that the docile creatures they see are in fact entire!

BITING

Biting is a classic form of dominant behaviour typical of an entire. He will nip and nibble at a mare to find out if she is ready to receive his attentions, and will grip her strongly by her neck with his teeth when covering her; and he will attack other colts with his teeth during a fight. Even in a domestic situation, their nibbling and biting instinct remains strong – entires just don't seem able to resist trying their teeth out on anything that happens to be passing! However, a young colt's nudging and nibbling will soon turn into full-scale biting, and the entire must learn right from the outset that this is unacceptable behaviour. Colts do not grow out of biting

– if anything, they grow *into* it and their nibbling behaviour becomes very much worse; so act as soon as your colt becomes nippy.

The traditional way of dealing with a biting horse is to slap it over the nose or to pinch it as soon as it tries to bite, or straight afterwards. However, it is impossible to react fast enough to deliver the blow at exactly the right moment, because to be effective, the horse must feel the consequences of his actions at the same moment that he commits the crime. A raised hand only ever seems to result in the horse tossing his head high out of reach and risks him becoming headshy, and with an entire, it may well result in him rearing above you. Besides, you want to raise your hand to the horse's face for a number of reasons in his future training, usually as a reward, so it is not a good idea to make him shy of it now.

There is a simple and effective way to teach a stallion or any other horse that biting is wrong, without him ever seeing you raise a hand to punish his behaviour. Put a headcollar on the horse and grip one side of it as you stroke his face; keep a firm hold on the headcollar, but don't restrict the horse's movement – as with halter-breaking, he must be free to behave badly so that you can take the opportunity to school him. When he makes a move to bite, push his face sharply out of the way with the hand holding the headcollar – then bring his head back to you just as quickly and stroke it again. The message you are trying to get across is the same as in so many other aspects of his training: when you're with me and behaving well, everything is pleasant for you; be naughty, and you will suffer the consequences of your own actions. By bringing the horse's head back to you after you have scolded him for biting, you remain the 'good guy', reassuring him that you bear no grudges and are still his friend, thus backing up the negative effects of your schooling with positive 'reward'. After a few repetitions this becomes a black-and-white situation in the horse's mind: when he is good, all is well, but life becomes unpleasant for him when he tries to bite. He has therefore been put in a position where he is accountable for his own actions.

It is very important that it is *your* decision, and not his, to bring his head back towards you. It shows him that it is *you* who controls situation, and makes it clear to him that even though you had to make him realise his mistake last time, you don't hold it against him and you won't hold grudges. If he attempts to bite again, he will get knocked sharply back again, and then be made to return under *your* conditions for his reward. You must be consistent and repeat the process every single time he tries to bite, whether or not he actually makes contact.

When you think he has learned the lesson, put it to the test by turning your back towards him (whilst still keeping an eye on him). Get close so you offer a tempting target, and make it easy for him to make that mistake and forget his manners if he's planning to. At the slightest nibble, jab your elbow back so that you bump his nose sharply off course – then turn round and renew your friendship with him by rubbing him between his eyes. As the final test, try putting your fingers into the horse's mouth and rubbing his gums: if you have schooled him properly, he will turn down this heaven-sent opportunity to bite, and will do so every time you try it, from that moment on!

THE FLEHMEN RESPONSE

This is typical stallion behaviour, although mares and geldings can also be seen doing it in response to a strong smell or taste. The extended neck and head and the curled upper lip are quite distinctive. It may be an indication of pain: mares may do it as they go into labour, and some horses if they are suffering from colic.

REARING

One habit to which entires are naturally inclined is rearing. While this is normally quite unacceptable behaviour for a ridden horse, for a stallion it is one of his party tricks, and those who keep entires must accept that from time to time they almost certainly *will* rear. It is part of the courtship ritual and something a stallion is much more inclined to do than any mare or gelding. There is a time and a place for everything, however, so analyse the stallion's reasons for rearing and act accordingly. Thus, is he specifically using it against you to get his own way, or is he simply showing off to his mares? The latter is natural and therefore forgivable to a certain extent. If, however, he is challenging *you*, maybe even turning to 'box' with his front legs as he would another horse, then you need to regain the upper hand in your relationship before somebody gets hurt.

A stallion is generally strong and well balanced enough to rear without risking a fall backwards, but it does nonetheless show a lack of respect and an assertion of his superiority which must be checked before it affects other aspects of his behaviour. Rearing is, after all, one of the most truly effective ways of asserting power and authority, as it puts the handler in such a helpless and vulnerable position.

REARING SOLUTIONS

As the horse stands up, he must inevitably expose his most vulnerable areas: his belly, chest and inner thighs. These soft areas are prime targets for wild cats and dogs when they hunt the wild horse down, and he is instinctively protective of them. The most effective way of curing a rearer is therefore to hit him hard under the belly with a piece of rope or the lash end of a whip as he stands up. This can be done either by a capable rider from above if the horse rears while ridden, or by the handler if the horse does it in hand. Such treatment will quickly discourage the stallion from exposing his vulnerable areas in such a way again, and it is usually only necessary to do this once

▲ This stallion is quite clearly showing off to these mares; for him it is a natural reaction. Don't confuse this with aggressive behaviour

or twice before the horse gets the message.

The traditional method of hitting a rearer over the head is barbaric and entirely misinformed, and what is more, it rarely works, mainly because the horse is an 'into-pressure' animal, as previously explained. Also, it is only possible to reach the top of his head when he is ridden, and not when he rears in hand, and it merely confirms to the horse that it is the rider who is responsible for his discomfort and makes him doubly determined to remove you. When he is hit under the

▲ This is not a problem horse, it is a stallion behaving perfectly normally! If you are not sure that you can handle this sort of behaviour calmly, reasonably and effectively, don't even think about keeping an entire. In this case a young stallion is being led past fields of other horses (including mares and other colts) so that Max can school any bad behaviour as it arises

belly, he does not associate it with the rider on top, besides which he can be disciplined in this way when ridden or led.

Bear in mind that in this case we have to do with a very specific type of rearer here: the stallion seeking to dominate. If an ordinary ridden horse begins to rear, the cause is entirely different and he should be treated sympathetically. Since such behaviour is invariably pain related; he must therefore not be punished because he is almost certainly desperately trying to tell you that something is wrong.

AGGRESSION

Stallions are naturally territorial and 'house-proud', and while this makes them a joy to muck out because all their droppings are usually in one place, it may lead them to be defensive about their stable. Thus, if a stallion becomes aggressive in his box, it is probably because he is 'chasing' you off his territory, indicating that he doesn't really see you as the boss; it shows a lack of respect which must be dealt with immediately.

First, see if there are any common factors which may give him an ulterior motive for being aggressive towards you: for example, does it happen when he's just covered a mare and his testosterone level is very high? Have you been handling an in-season mare? Have you been sloppy in your handling habits or started feeding him titbits? If he does it when you approach with tack, are you sure he isn't in some sort of pain which makes being ridden an uncomfortable chore? Is he on too rich a diet for his workload?

Once you have eliminated all the common-sense options, work on reasserting your authority out of the box first. Tune him into your body language with a pressure halter (as pictured and described above). Make him keep his head to you and 'join up' (see Stage 4), then work over all his vulnerable areas and pick up his feet — remember, this is psychologically 'disabling' for a horse. Back in the box, use aggressive body language to get him to back away from you and insist that he keeps his head to you as established in your join-up sessions.

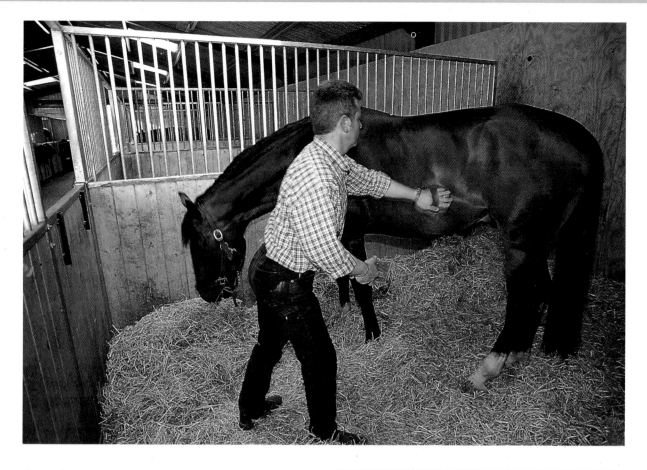

▲ Good manners in the box are essential. It is a misconception that stallions need tying up, as they are very sociable and like to be touched

TEARING RUGS

This is another example of natural territorial behaviour, and there isn't really a quick solution. The stallion feels he must make everything his personal property and biting is a favourite habit, so give him the oldest, toughest rugs you can find and allow him to imprint them with his smell. You can even put them on the floor and allow him to kick them around the box for an hour or two. When he has worn the rug for a few days and it begins to smell more familiar, the habit usually wears off, so don't be in too much of a hurry to take the rug away to clean and repair! Stallions are more comfortable with things they are really familiar with, so always use the same rug; but if he needs a new one, you will probably have to let him subject it to the above ritual. This behaviour is quite common; however, if it seems unduly persistent, consider discomfort as a possible cause.

STAGE 5
CHECKLIST

- Ask yourself if you can do a stallion justice.
- Halter-break your young colt properly.
- Don't be in awe of an entire. He is an intelligent animal and will respond to correct training.
- Make allowances for natural instincts, but never cheeky behaviour.
- Good behaviour on the ground will invariably be reflected in the stallion's ridden work.
- Allow him to live as natural a lifestyle as possible.
- Be quick to nip potentially bad habits in the bud.
- Familiarity breeds contempt, so guard against developing sloppy handling habits. Be as disciplined with yourself as you are with the horse.
- Make sure that every person who handles the stallion is competent and consistent.
- Establish a solid routine. The entire should be in no doubt as to when he is going for a hack, and when he has to cover a mare, so he can behave accordingly.

STAGE 6
ADOLESCENT ANXIETIES
Age: 18 months to 2½ years

It has always surprised me that horse owners wait until a horse is three or even four years old before starting to work with him; even more surprising is that they believe they are doing him a favour by leaving him to 'mature'. In fact there is nothing particularly special about him being three – it is simply the age when physically a horse is strong enough to carry a rider for short periods of time. Think of all the things a child learns before it goes to school; basic discipline, communication skills and a few social graces make him a far more confident and receptive pupil when the time comes, and it is the same for the horse. Actually carrying a rider is one of the last pieces of the jigsaw to slot into place, and there is a great deal you should do with a youngster before this stage.

By the time the horse is eighteen months old he should have respect for you and your personal space, he should be properly halter-broken, he should pick up his feet on request, stand to be tied up and groomed, and allow you to handle him all over. If he is properly halter-broken there is no reason why he should not load into and out of a horsebox or trailer without a fuss, either. Good preparation will boost the confidence of the rider as well as the horse, so that the whole backing process becomes just another small step in the continuous process of schooling the horse, rather than a major event in itself.

▶ It may be too early for physical stress, but mental stimulation is another matter. Now is the time to get your horse used to as many experiences as possible, such as loading into both lorries and trailers

INTRODUCING EQUIPMENT

▲ Mutual trust and respect has been established through join-up. This horse is ready to accept anything that Max suggests, even if it goes against his natural instinct

▼ Once the tack is on, he will probably want to investigate it; sniffing and licking is his way of gathering information

Once the horse has taken the decision that he wants to be with you, you will have gained his unconditional trust and respect. He will follow at your heels and enjoy what he now regards as the privilege of your company, and as far as he is concerned, such a decision is pretty well irreversible unless you act unreasonably and abuse his trust. He has accepted you as a friend and acknowledged you as a leader, and this puts you in a strong position to start asking favours and introducing various pieces of equipment. To the horse they may look and smell very strange, but if you say they are OK, then he will be prepared to accept them. At eighteen months to two-and-a-half years a horse is still too young and skeletally immature to take the weight of a rider and be expected to perform – unless he is a Thoroughbred racehorse. However, at this stage he can certainly be accustomed to the equipment that he will eventually wear, so that he becomes relaxed and completely comfortable with it. By putting on boots, bandages, rugs and all the various items of tack, you will teach him complete familiarity with every aspect of the breaking-in process apart from actually backing him.

I always begin where I left off after joining up with the horse (see Stage 4), in the round pen; however, if you haven't got a pen, then corner off a small area of your field or school with bales, jump poles or any other effective barrier that leaves you with an area of about 20 metres square to work in. The horse must be loose, and free to react instinctively; any physical restraint, such as a lunge line, links you too directly with him. He must seek your company voluntarily, and if things go wrong, he must not associate any unpleasant experience with you. Furthermore if he is loose, you will be forced to use body language as your sole means of communication (see Stage 1), and to watch his more carefully.

Act slowly and alone. Although many

▶ The benefits of join-up. This horse stands and faces Max, awaiting the next move. He shows no fear, just calm curiosity

people have logical reasons for the traditional method of enlisting a helper, technically this may be interpreted as ganging up on the horse, and implies that you expect things to go wrong! Be assured that the horse will not go back on his side of the bargain unless you cause him to change his mind about you. If the horse does not trust you enough to allow you to do what you want, then you must wait until your relationship improves before attempting to go any further.

I also feel that the 'softly, softly' approach is a mistake often made when introducing young horses to new equipment. Too many people sidle up and quietly try to 'sneak' a strange object such as a rug or saddle onto the horse's back, thinking that they are being tactful. In fact all they are doing is taking the horse by surprise and giving him the idea that there is something to worry about! This sort of timid approach nearly always saps the horse's confidence and confirms his suspicion that there is something to be afraid of, so he will jump and react accordingly.

Do exactly the opposite, and it will have the opposite effect: march up to the horse with the equipment, allow him to smell and investigate it, reassure him with your voice and place it firmly where you want it. If the horse jumps and runs away, then so be it. If he realises that he is not trapped and can move away if he wants to, his panic will subside much more quickly than if he is restricted or tied up, and you can try again.

▶ Act slowly and alone, leaving the horse free to react. It must be *his* decision that he stays and allows you to do what you want; he should not be forced to do so

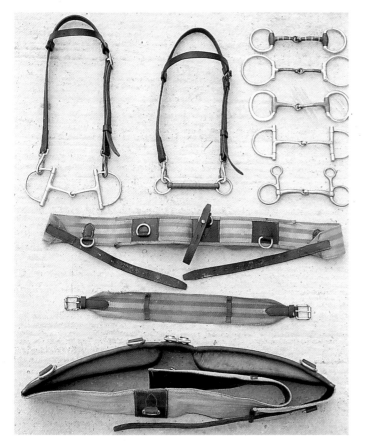

◀ Equipment should be simple, comfortable and preferably old! The snaffle bits clip on to the bridle headpiece to make them easier to take on and off, and there is no need for a noseband or reins at this stage. A breastplate will stop the surcingle slipping back; it also introduces the sort of restriction the horse will feel over his chest and back when he wears a rug for the first time

▼ The horse learns to tolerate new equipment in the stable first. The hanging bags are all part of the process intended to make the horse less sensitive about the unusual, and so less likely to succumb to his natural instincts which would be to flee

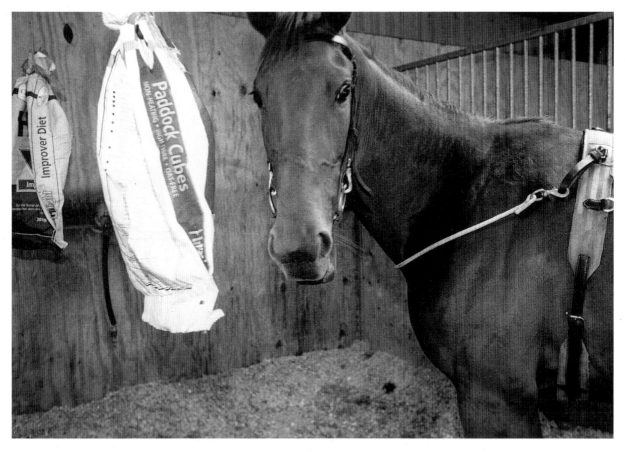

BOOTS AND BANDAGES

Even if you don't intend your horse to wear boots or bandages, it is sensible to teach him to accept them. The whole process is part of a bigger picture which aims to build up the horse's trust and confidence as much as possible. Consider your early lessons at school: you probably haven't used half the things you learned, such as mathematical equations or French translation, but the discipline of learning them and the mental stimulation was part of a wider learning process and contributed to mental awareness and logical thinking – and confidence above all. It is essential that the young horse believes that he can cope with whatever situation you present him with. Also, the less alarm he feels about having things around his legs now, the less likely he is to take fright at other items of tack or clothing such as long-reins or the leg straps on a rug.

You should have been handling your horse's legs regularly for several months by this stage, so putting boots on should not cause any problems. However, initially the horse may not like the feeling of them on his legs as he tries to move, and only experience in the longer term will teach him that this is nothing to worry about. Bandages are softer and conform to the leg better than boots, but the process of putting them on and off needs time and patience, so make sure the horse is used to boots first. Again, you may not intend to use bandages, but sooner or later the horse will have to be dressed for travelling, or he may need stable bandages to support an injury, and these are not ideal circumstances for him to experience them for the first time.

BUILDING UP CONFIDENCE

The technique for introducing new equipment to a young horse remains the same no matter what the item is – a surcingle on his back will not feel so very different from a saddle to him, although its significance to the handler is much greater! However, it does make sense to start with simple equipment and to introduce more complicated items progressively as the horse's confidence increases. Begin by putting a weigh-tape or soft rope round his middle while you are grooming him in the stable, gradually drawing it tight, then releasing, every time you handle him. Flop the rope or

▼ When a horse continues to eat while wearing new equipment then he must be feeling relaxed about it!

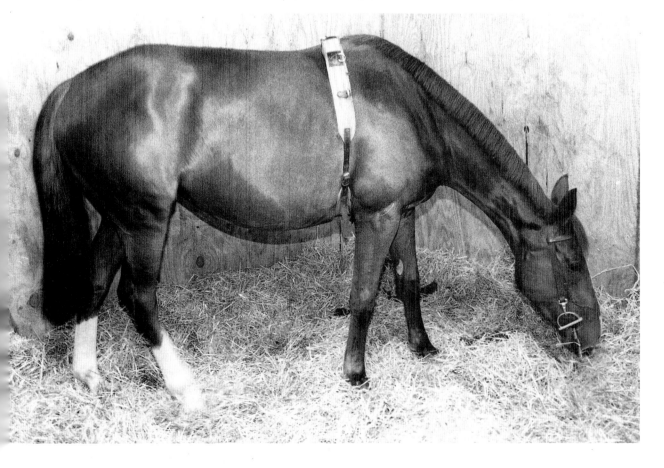

◀ Allow the horse to investigate and explore everything both before you put it on, and afterwards. Never punish him for chewing it or testing it with his teeth, or pawing at it on the ground at this stage, because by doing so he is putting his own mind at rest

▼ When the horse is completely comfortable with the different items of equipment in the stable, the next stage of his education is to let him run loose in your pen, school or safe enclosed area. He must be quite free to trot or canter about, and to explore and experiment with the tack

▲ The 'softly, softly' approach is often used when introducing young horses to new equipment and this is a mistake: it is better to just march up and show them there's nothing to be afraid of!

▲ (Above right) The horse should be loose, as he is here, so that if he wants to run away, he can. His trust in you and his curiosity in the equipment will soon bring him back

▶ Don't be in too much of a hurry to get the saddle done up. Practise putting it on and taking it off until the horse accepts it as routine

tape over his back and dangle it over his neck until he is completely used to it, then exchange the tape for a real surcingle and do the same thing.

Don't actually do up the buckles of the surcingle until you have gauged the horse's reaction to it. Some horses are inclined to feel trapped, and panic when they feel a tight, immovable band around them for the first time. Respect his flight instincts and be sympathetic, allowing him plenty of time to become accustomed to the sensation. Positioning the surcingle and doing it up is just the beginning – you must then take it on and off many times until he is completely bored by the whole procedure. Next, leave it on for an hour or two at a time; when you reach this stage, use a breastplate attachment to prevent it slipping back, because this would alarm him unnecessarily. It can be useful to have some hay in the stable, as a guide to the horse's state of mind – if he continues to eat while you handle him, then he must be feeling relaxed!

SADDLING UP

Once the horse is used to the surcingle, it is a relatively small step to exchange it for a saddle. The horse has no idea of the significance that a saddle will come to have in his life, and he should just view it as a variation on the surcingle at this stage. It is ironic that the very place we want to sit on the horse is exactly where he would be attacked by a predator, so it is essential to do all you can to help him overcome every bit of alarm or apprehension about being handled in this area before he is actually backed.

Use an older saddle if possible, because when you allow the horse to sniff and investigate the new object he may nibble or paw at it – and he should not be prevented from doing this at this stage, because it is his way of putting his own mind at rest, and it will ultimately make *your* life easier if he is relaxed and confident with the equipment. Approach confidently, place the saddle high over the withers and slide it

backwards to the correct place; and do this several times over several days, until the horse is used to it. There is no reason why he should object in any way at all if he has been properly prepared. Attach the girth and do it up *firmly*; the horse should be used to this if you have prepared him by using a surcingle.

A word of warning: trying to be 'nice' by doing the girth loosely can be counter-productive, and even dangerous if the horse does take exception to it and buck; if the saddle slips back or underneath him, it would leave him with a very bad early memory, something you must avoid at all costs. It would take you months to overcome the resulting fear and suspicion – so take no chances, and girth up tightly from the start. Work from both sides of the horse, and make putting the saddle on and taking it off a part of your grooming routine.

PUTTING ON THE BRIDLE

I generally use an old-fashioned copper and black-iron bit to start with; from the horse's point of view it is a warmer metal with a less obnoxious taste than stainless steel. There are also many copper or copper-based bits on the market. It is important to choose a bit which suits the conformation of your horse's mouth and tongue; while a thicker mouthpiece exerts less pressure, a thinner one may be easier for a youngster to accept initially. As always, treat each horse as an individual, and remember that until he is around five years old, his mouth and teeth will keep changing. Of course, if his teeth are sharp or sore he will be unwilling to accept any bit at all, so have them checked by a qualified equine dentist. It is worth travelling many miles to find a good one – after all, the

◀ The horse must be loose and free to react instinctively when he is first introduced to new equipment. Any physical restraint, such as a lunge line, links you too directly with the horse – the idea that when *he* moves, *it* moves, will be completely alien to him and may bring all his primitive flight instincts to the fore. Be there to offer reassurance

◀ This youngster is quite calmly running about loose wearing a saddle; the stirrups have been deliberately left swinging, so he gets used to the feel of them hitting his sides

▶ Practice makes perfect! The horse must learn to open his mouth for the bit, which he will only do if you make the experience as easy and stress-free as possible

▲ This is where things can start to go wrong if you have not
spent sufficient time handling vulnerable areas such as the
head, and persuading the horse to be less sensitive about
your touching them. Equally important is a comfortable bit.
Make sure, too, that nothing is tight or chafes around the
ears, and that the browband is loose enough

horse's teeth should only need seeing to once a year if they are done properly, and it will make all the difference to his enjoyment of life.

Because the horses I start are so used to having their heads and ears handled, and because I have always made a point of rubbing my fingers around their mouth and gums from an early age, fitting the bit is never a problem. I usually leave them to wear it in the stable for a short while every day. The bridle should be fitted without a noseband or reins, and must be quite loose around the ears — horses can be made chronically headshy as a result of a bridle which pinches around the ears, as I have seen happen myself.

RUGS

Very often one of the most frightening experiences for the young horse is having a rug put on, not the saddle. This is hardly surprising, since a rug is so big and flapping, with ticklish leg straps and buckles and which swathes his whole body from chest to tail — as a sensitive flight animal, he is bound to feel trapped and uncomfortable to begin with. Bear in mind also that rugs can't be done up as tightly, or fitted as securely as a saddle, and that they are inclined to slip — so don't take any chances on the first occasion you put a rug on your horse.

Start by draping a small blanket or towel over the horse's back, and secure it under the surcingle. Once he is used to the feeling of this over his back in the stable, move on to a cotton sheet, again secured by the surcingle; then a light stable rug. As always, let the horse sniff the rug before you put it on, and rub a corner of it all over his body. Once you have made the decision to put the rug over the horse you must not let yourself be put off if he takes fright — so if he moves away, you must move with him; put it against his skin and keep it there until he stops and you can slide it further onto his back and fasten it. He must not be allowed to think that shying away will make you back off and so win him the easy option.

If the horse is really anxious, or if he has had a bad experience in the past, leave the rug in his box overnight for him to investigate at his leisure, and drape it over yourself every time you handle him. The smell will then become more familiar, and he will associate the rug with a pleasant experience, such as being fussed, fed or groomed by you. Remember that

he gets his confidence from *you*, so pretend that it is really of no consequence at all, and be confident as you throw the rug over his back, even if you suspect he will shy away. It is no good relaxing once it is on, either, since the anticipation of the rug flying though the air and landing on his back is the most traumatic part of the experience for the horse; so you need to take it on and off many times to make him realise that his anticipation is far worse than the reality.

The sheer weight of a large New Zealand-type rug is enough to frighten a horse, so to begin with, put it on in the stable where he can't run off and frighten himself when he realises that this thing is following him! It is not unusual for young horses to stand rooted to the spot when they first start wearing a rug, convinced that they can't move. When you *do* turn the horse out in a rug for the first time, do so in a fairly small area so that you can catch hold of him and reassure him if he reacts violently.

STAGE 6

CHECKPOINTS

- ■ Start early — don't wait until a horse is three years old to accustom it to tack and equipment.

- ■ Establish a good join-up first, so that the horse knows where to go for reassurance.

- ■ Allow the horse to investigate all new equipment.

- ■ Avoid the 'softly, softly' technique — your horse will gain confidence from a more direct approach.

- ■ Don't back off when introducing new equipment, even if the horse does look apprehensive. He must not 'train' you into leaving him alone.

- ■ Introduce tack in the stable first, and leave it on until the horse is used to it.

- ■ Don't risk the saddle slipping — always use a breastplate.

- ■ Tack up from both sides.

- ■ Even if the horse does not need them, teach him to wear boots.

- ■ Make sure the horse's teeth and back are comfortable before introducing a bit or saddle; you do not want him to associate them with pain.

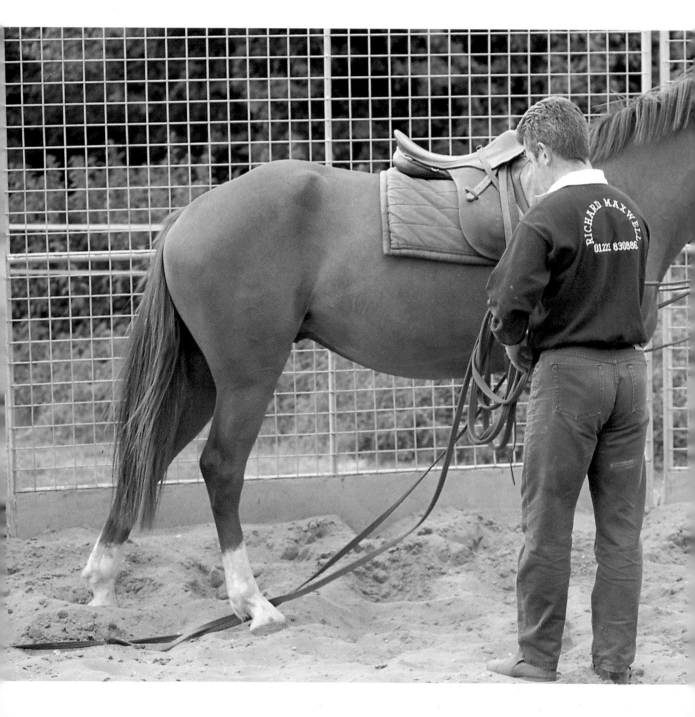

TO
REIN Age: 2 to 3 years

Familiarising the horse with everything he will have to cope with later, when he is ridden, is the key to building his confidence and minimising potential problems, and there is still plenty you can do from on the ground to prepare the young horse for when he is eventually backed. So far his work has been mentally stimulating rather than physically demanding, and this is the way it should stay if he is to enjoy each new stage as it is introduced. Long-reining can be made physically demanding for a more advanced horse, but for the youngster it is simply part of a learning curve, albeit a very important part.

THE LONG-TERM BENEFITS

Long-reining is by far the best way to introduce the young horse to the feel of pressure on the bit, and to teach him the basic aids to slow down and change direction before he has the added stress of carrying a rider. It may be obvious to the rider that a pull on the left rein means go left and a pull on the right rein means go right, but it certainly is not to the horse! His body will not necessarily follow his nose and the unfamiliar pressure from metal or hard rubber on what

is still a highly sensitive mouth can upset him, especially if it comes at the same time as carrying a rider for the first time. On no account do you want him to think that being ridden is an uncomfortable experience, so take one step at a time and use long-reining to teach him to turn and stop before you get on. By doing so, you are reducing the chances of anything going wrong at the backing stage.

Long-reining also teaches the horse to accept the

◀ The more paranoid he is about feeling the lines around his legs, the more you should do it to him, until he learns that there is nothing to fear. As well as giving both you and the youngster one less thing to worry about, it will certainly make him a safer ride in the future

that his objections are fully justified; so help him to confront his fear, rather than avoiding the issue. While in a familiar and secure area, deliberately allow the reins to drop around the horse's feet, talking to him all the time. He may well not like the feeling of lines round his legs or feet at first, but if you have done your homework and handled his legs regularly, he will soon realise that this is just a variation on the same theme.

As you progress with the long-reining, the horse will get used to 'listening backwards' and thinking about what is going on behind him, and this is an excellent preparation for carrying a rider. Also, although you will still use your voice to give directions, the horse will have to start transferring his attention from you to the bit, and take instructions from your aids rather than just concentrating on your voice or body language. Furthermore, by using the long-reins against the horse's sides you are introducing the concept of leg aids, and this will make it easier for him to accept and understand the first basic aids his rider will give him.

WHY NOT LUNGE?

Less experienced handlers tend not to long-rein because they worry about getting in a tangle, and many teach a young horse to lunge instead. Lungeing a horse is fine as a form of exercise, and to teach the horse balance, and obedience to the voice and whip. However, it does not introduce a young horse to the all-important feel of the rider's hands on the other end of each rein, nor does it teach him to accept their guidance. Nor does it imitate the effect of the outside leg in the same way as long-reining.

And lungeing a horse which has 'joined up' with you has another, significant complication: you may have spent weeks teaching him that when he stops and turns in and comes up to you, he will get a reward – but when you lunge him, every time he tries to come to you, you punish him by sending him away with a whip. Inevitably this will confuse him, and spoil any degree of join-up you may have achieved.

feel of tack flapping around his legs and against his sides. This is all part of the process of helping the flight animal to become less wary and sensitive, a concern which has formed the basis of the horse's training to date. Thus, don't worry should the reins drop too low around the horse's legs – if this happens, he must learn to deal with it, and the sooner the better. In fact it is the ideal opportunity to turn what seems like a mistake into a valuable learning experience for the horse, and for it to have a positive rather than a negative effect.

If you are constantly worried about how the horse will react if he *does* get in a tangle with the reins, he will sense this and it will upset him, and will convince him

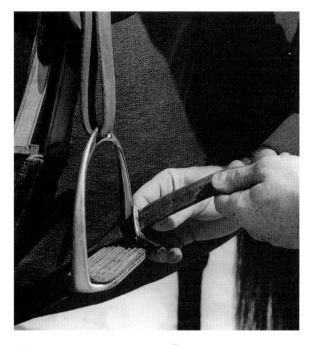

▲▼ Fasten the stirrups beneath his belly with an old stirrup leather (as pictured) to keep them in position, and pass each lunge-rein through the stirrup iron and up to the bit-ring; this will stop them dropping too low

BEFORE YOU START...

Remember that anything new should be introduced to the horse as an 'extra' at the end of a normal schooling session, when he is relaxed, confident and in 'learning mode'. So start where you left off, by working him in the pen or enclosed area, using the equipment in which he will eventually be ridden, that is, a snaffle bridle and saddle. The horse should work with the stirrups pulled down fairly short, but so they hang just below the saddle flaps. In this way he gets used to feeling them move against his sides, and so when he is backed, feeling the rider's legs and feet will come as less of a surprise.

The horse is used to being directed by pressure on his nose from the headcollar, but he has never experienced pressure on his mouth, even though he is now used to wearing a bit; it is this pressure which he must accept before backing. Because I never long-rein until the horse is joined-up and has learned to

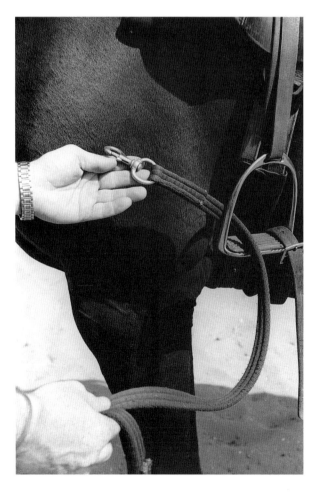

overcome his instinct to lean into pressure (see Stage 3), I feel it is more beneficial to attach the reins directly to the bit. If anything happens, I know the horse will stop in response to the pressure and bring his head to me. It is obviously undesirable to pull or damage a young horse's mouth in any way, however, so if you have any doubts about your own ability or your horse's reaction to the bit, then long-rein the horse with the reins attached to a lungeing cavesson initially, or just attach a line to each side of the noseband of a headcollar provided that the horse has been properly halter-broken (see Stage 3).

INTRODUCING LONG-REINS

Although I usually prefer to work alone with the horse, on a one-to-one basis, when introducing long-reins it can be useful to have an assistant by his head to reassure and guide him, so that you do not have to put too much pressure on his mouth while he gets used to the idea.

Clip a lunge-rein onto the bit-ring on the off side, and pass it through the stirrup and over the saddle to the near side. Don't bring the line behind the horse's quarters just yet. For now, remain at the horse's shoulder, with your assistant if you have one. Attach the second lunge-rein to the near side in the same way, but instead of passing it over the saddle, keep hold of it after passing it through the stirrup.

Ask the horse to walk on, staying at his shoulder and keeping the lunge lines coiled so that they are no longer than ordinary reins. Gradually take up the lightest of contacts on the reins, and if the horse appears comfortable, slowly increase the distance between yourself and him. Initially he won't understand why he can feel something on his off side when he can quite clearly see you on the near side! As his confidence increases you can increase the distance between you, but stay on one side so that he can still see you.

▼ With a horse that trusts you, restraint is not necessary even when long-reining in open spaces

With the outside rein still lying over the saddle rather than round the horse's quarters, ask the horse to halt by using your usual command combined with a slight squeeze on the reins. Your assistant can move in front of the horse to reinforce the message and make it as obvious as possible what you want him to do. Praise him enthusiastically the moment he halts, and release the pressure on his mouth immediately. Then ask him to walk and halt again, and as you keep repeating the process, put less emphasis on your body language and more on the rein aid. Once the horse starts to transfer his attention from you to the bit, change sides and try on the other rein.

Use of the voice and body language will help you to communicate with the horse until he becomes accustomed to taking directions from the long-reins. Remember that he considers his two sides independently, and finds it genuinely hard to transfer what he has learned on one side, to the other; so don't get frustrated if he appears to be deliberately awkward on one side, but just work through the resistance calmly and patiently.

Don't demand perfection – once he has a vague understanding of walking and halting on both reins, he has done enough for one day.

ENDING THE SESSION

When the horse has stopped, coil the reins up as you walk to his head. With an older horse which is used to being long-reined, I just drop the reins on the ground and walk up to the horse and unclip them. This is unconventional, but if you have taken all the steps described so far to gain your horse's respect and to overcome his flight instinct, he should not panic even if he does take a step and feel the reins around his legs. It is on occasions such as this that you will reap the rewards of the time you have spent establishing the horse's confidence, handling his vulnerable areas and building up his trust in you; so rather than panicking and trying to run away in times of crisis, the joined-up horse's first reaction to danger is to stop and let *you* sort things out for him.

◄ It is quite likely that he will stick his tongue out and make faces as he feels the unfamiliar pressure on the bit, so keep using strong body language and a familiar vocal command to get the message across, rather than pulling harder

EARLY LESSONS

▲ With a horse which is accustomed to long-reining, dropping the lines and walking to his head is a sign that the session is over

Have your second long-reining session fairly soon after the first – the next day or even later the same day is ideal. Take the horse into an enclosed area and start with your usual loose schooling routine, then add the lunge-reins and practise 'stop and start' as before. When the horse seems happy and you no longer need an assistant to achieve what you want, gradually drop further and further back towards the horse's quarters, taking the outside lunge-rein with you so that it lies across the horse's croup rather than the saddle. From this position it should be quite easy to drop the outside rein around the horse's quarters. You should be standing sufficiently far away and still slightly to one side,

so if the horse kicks out you are well out of range.

Keep walking and halting the horse, letting out the reins until you have distanced yourself for the full length of them and are standing at the centre of the circle, with the horse walking round you as if positioned for lungeing. Ask him to go forwards into trot and allow him to canter if he offers it, combining your voice and body language with a flick of the outside rein behind his quarters to encourage him forwards. Remember that your own body position will influence the horse just as it does when he works loose, so beware of inadvertently 'blocking' his forward movement by getting in front of his eyeline.

To initiate the turn, take up a contact with the outside rein and drop the contact on the inside rein. Use your body language to block the horse by stepping ahead of his eye-line, then drop back to hip level and drive him from behind. Use the fence of the manège to help you; don't attempt a turn like this on the open side of the school until the horse understands what you are asking

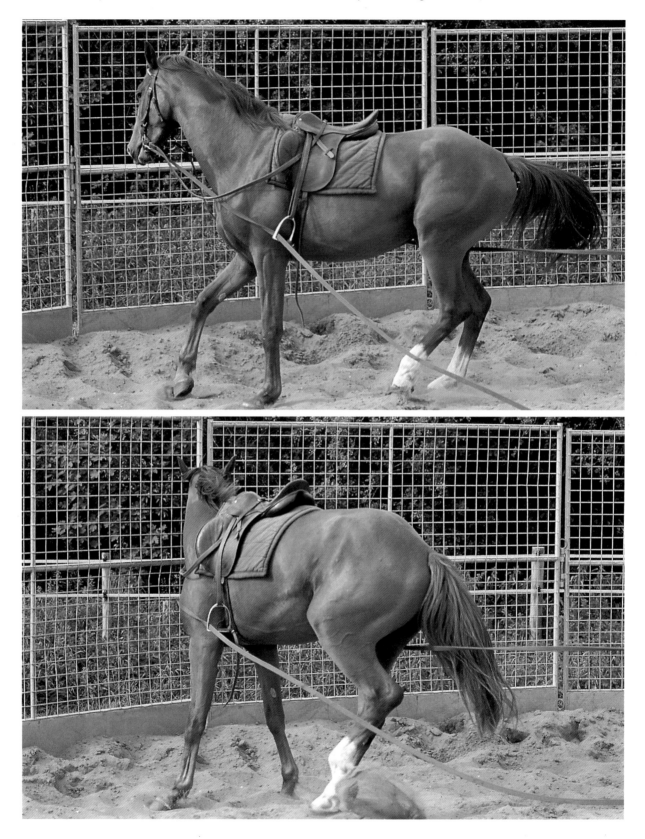

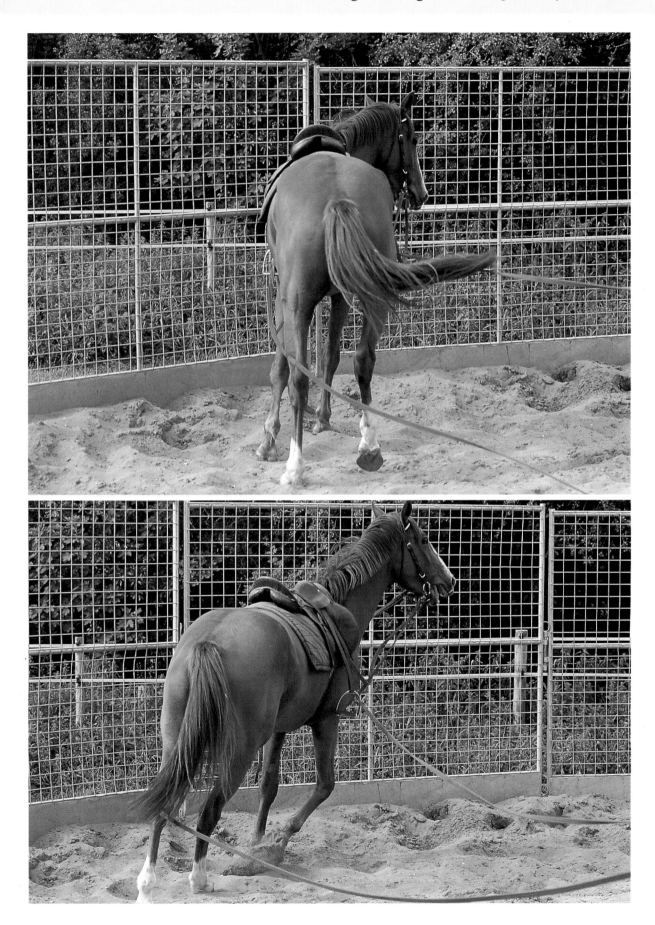

▲ Drop the reins slowly over the horse's back end; his ears will indicate how much, and where his attention is focused

▶ Long-lining (-reining) encourages self-carriage and balance without the hindrance of a rider

▼ Don't be in too much haste to get the lines behind the horse's quarters; it can cause him great anxiety

In a round pen or enclosed schooling area, the horse will be guided more by the walls and track of his regular circle than by the rein aids, making both your lives easier. Keep practising transitions between halt, walk, trot and canter, initially using body language and the voice, then transferring the emphasis to the rein aids until the horse is paying more attention to the feel of the reins on the bit than to you personally. Be careful to keep both reins very loose – their weight alone will be enough to guide the horse, and you should not need to pull.

▲▼ Walking behind the horse is a more classical long-reining position, and allows you to give more subtle and accurate rein aids. It is from this position that you will teach the horse how to turn, because you can step around his quarters and change sides easily. The inside rein automatically becomes the outside, and you can send the horse off in the other direction

WORKING FROM BEHIND

While the horse is in walk or halt, you can move from your position at the centre of the circle and gradually drop further behind him, so that he has a less clear view of you and must listen to the directions given from behind via the reins. Vary your work between standing at the centre of the circle, and giving instructions from behind him (this will be restricted to walk and a little trot unless you are a very fast runner!).

TURNING TIPS

When you communicate to the horse that you want him to change direction, make sure he doesn't try to turn the wrong way. If he has joined up with you, he may try to bring his head to you and swing his quarters away, rather than turning on his haunches. This may work when he is loose in the pen, but he will get tangled up if he is wearing long-reins. Keep it slow and use the reins to encourage him to turn in the right direction.

I have always found that the horse quickly recognises the difference between long-reining and loose work in the pen, and he will put the 'joined-up' side of your relationship, which might normally cause him to stop and bring his head to you all the time, 'on hold' for the duration of the training session. Dressing him up in saddle, bridle and long-reins is like him picking up his briefcase and putting on a bowler hat, ready for work: it is a different scenario to join-up, and you are sending him different signals.

DEALING WITH PROBLEMS

The fear of the unknown is strong, and youngsters must be given the time and space to express themselves and investigate all new equipment. They may want to kick out at the long-reins or have a buck when they feel them against their sides, and it is important that the handler does not stifle this natural expression, or panic that things are going wrong — as we have already discovered throughout our relationship with the horse so far, the best way of teaching him that he has nothing to fear is to let him discover it for himself. If he does appear to be genuinely frightened rather than naturally

▼ This 'joined-up' horse is trying to evade facing an unfamiliar situation by coming to me. This must not be punished, but he must be calmly put back to work

apprehensive, then the fault is yours. You are moving too fast for that particular animal, or you have left room for doubt in other areas of his training, and need to go back a step.

If for any reason your horse reacts violently, or should you encounter unforeseen problems when long-reining, drop the outside rein and use the inside rein to turn the horse in to face you, which any joined-up horse will be inclined to do anyway. Walk up to him and rub him between his eyes, talking to him until he calms down and responds to your reassurances.

By now the horse should clearly understand that you are the comfort zone. It is a very good idea to use the principles established with join-up in the pen (see Stage 4) to diffuse a potentially difficult situation — but — make sure you only praise, reward and reassure the horse *when he needs or deserves it*. Remember that

▼ This young filly wears a roller for the first time and is reacting as expected. The line is attached but is not preventing her expressing herself

stopping work and coming to you is his reward. If you constantly praise him in anticipation of a problem rather than as a result of good behaviour, or regularly use praise to calm the horse down when he is naughty, you are in fact condoning the negative rather than rewarding the positive.

WORKING OVER POLES

When the horse has accepted the basic rules of long-reining, work over poles may be introduced. Long-reining him over and around poles on the ground adds a new dimension to his training and puts yet another piece in his educational jigsaw puzzle. Start by long-reining him over and round a single pole, then add two or three more so that he must walk down a line of poles and between each one of them. As well as giving

▶ Working a horse over and around poles adds interest and improves co-ordination. It is sensible to accustom the horse to poles in-hand before using them during long-reining exercises

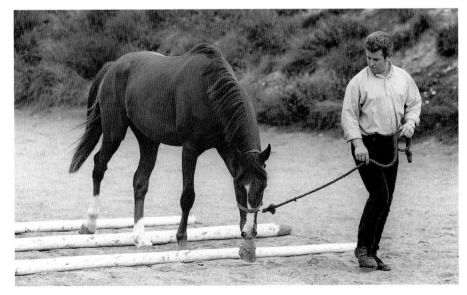

him something else to think about, the horse must look where he is putting his feet, take his directions mostly from the reins and make his own way forwards without you at his head.

While the horse is perfectly capable of walking over poles, doing it all by himself presents a psychological barrier – suddenly this long-reining business is not so simple! If he wants to stop and sniff, let him do so, but try not to let him back off the poles. The only way out is forwards, and you must behave as if there are no other options.

You may be surprised at just how unco-ordinated young horses are – many don't even know where their back legs are – and he may be a little shocked if he knocks or treads on a pole. Stay calm and reassure the horse while he thinks it through. I prefer youngsters not to wear boots because they need to learn where their legs are, to 'feel' the poles and learn from experience. They are only working in walk and are not generally shod at this age, so are highly unlikely to damage themselves, and I feel that the disadvantages of wearing boots outweigh the advantages.

OUT AND ABOUT

Long-reining your horse and watching how he works will give you useful clues as to the type of ridden horse he is going to be. It should now be clear if he favours one side or the other, which pace is his favourite, how bold or cautious he is by nature, and how ready he is to accept new ideas or adapt to certain situations.

Horses translate lessons learned on the ground to their ridden work very well, and the day is fast approaching when the young horse will be taken out with a rider on board. Preparation is everything, and it is not really fair on the horse to keep within the safe confines of a school for ever. If you have suitably quiet lanes or a busy yard or farm nearby, try long-reining the horse past as many obstacles as you can so that he has seen a few hazards. If he hesitates, encourage him to go forwards by using your voice and flicking the reins along his sides. This will help his understanding of the rider's leg aids at a later date, and reinforce the message that while you don't mind him hesitating to look and weigh up a situation, going back or refusing is not an option once you have asked him to do something.

STAGE 7
CHECKPOINTS

- Always carry out your first long-reining sessions in a small, enclosed area.

- Use the equipment the horse will be ridden in, and make sure he is comfortable wearing it.

- If the horse is unshod, it is more valuable to leave boots off and let him get used to the feel of the lines on his legs.

- Never pull on the horse's mouth – the weight of the loose long-reins should be sufficient to guide him.

- Long-rein with the reins attached to a headcollar if you are unsure of the horse's reactions to the bit.

- Let the horse dictate the pace. It is fine for him to canter in long-reins for short periods if he is comfortable doing so.

- The horse must be allowed to express himself, so don't panic if he kicks out at the long-reins initially.

- Don't expect perfection in one session: once the horse understands the concept of stopping and turning, that is probably enough for the day.

- Beware of blocking the horse's forward movement with your body position.

- Allow for the horse's lack of balance and co-ordination – keep the pace slow when turning or working him over poles.

- Use this opportunity to gather valuable information about your future riding horse's attitude, strengths and weaknesses.

STAGE 8
BACKING & RIDING AWAY

Age: 3 years and over

If the mutual trust and understanding between you and your horse is everything it should be by this stage, you should be looking forward to being able to ride him! It is appropriate that in this book only one chapter is devoted to actually backing the horse. This is because the preparation is the most important part, and that if that goes well, backing is the easy bit!

Very often it is the rider, not the horse, who is most anxious about the initial backing process. Backing a young horse for the first time really isn't the traumatic experience it is made out to be, and there will be no dramatic scenes or rodeos if the horse has been properly prepared. It is simply the next piece in the jigsaw, and the horse should be eager to learn where it fits. In fact he is in part broken already if he is happily carrying all the equipment he needs in order to be ridden, and is responding obediently to your commands to stop, start and turn; he just hasn't had a person on his back before.

Lessons must have been thorough and logical, and you should be certain that the horse has understood each stage before you move on to the next. If you have prepared him properly up to this stage, you should be confident that he will respond well to being backed. If you have any doubts, it may be a sign that either you or he are not ready. Remember that the unbacked horse has no negative thoughts associated with having a rider on his back: if all his previous learning experiences have been positive, then why should this be any different? To him it is just another day's work, with an added variation in his lesson time.

PREPARING FOR BACKING

WHEN TO BACK?

There is still some debate as to the 'right' age to back a horse. Thoroughbreds mature more quickly than some of the heavier breeds, and racehorses are backed as yearlings, but it is more usual to back a horse at three or four years old.

In fact the horse's frame is not generally mature enough to cope with 'proper' work until he is six; so until that time you are dealing more with his mind than his body. It is therefore just as well to ignore standard time limits and go with what feels right. I often find that a really bright young horse needs serious mental stimulation to keep him out of trouble, and that the sooner he is backed, the better, as it gives him something constructive to think about! Entire colts often fall into this category. On the other hand, a nervous or 'backward' youngster may benefit from being left a little longer to gain confidence in himself and his handler; to risk a misunderstanding at this stage would be a great pity. The unbacked horse has no reason to resent having a rider on board, so why give him one?

By this stage the horse should submit to every part of his body being handled; he should be well mannered and attentive to your requests; he should respect you and your personal space; he should stop, start and steer on long-reins and should have experienced traffic and a number of everyday hazards in hand. If he has done all this, then all that is missing is the rider!

WHERE TO BACK?

It is quite common for horses to be backed for the first time in their stable. This appears to be more for the rider's reassurance than the horse, and I think it is a bad idea. If you had an important lesson planned for a child, he is more likely to listen and concentrate in the classroom than in the playground — so take the horse out to his normal schooling environment to back him. This is the place which he associates with listening and learning, and after all, backing him is just another lesson. Consider, too, that in the stable there is nowhere to go if the horse *does* react violently, and this could be dangerous.

Moreover, the stable is the horse's territory, and he sees it as a place of rest and relaxation, not work. Remember the part which freedom of choice has had in your relationship with the horse to date: he has always been able to run if he is uncertain, but he stays with you because he wants to, and not because he has been forced to. This is part of the learning process, but it is only physically possible in an open space — and this must be safer for the rider than being trapped in a twelve-foot-square box with a panicking youngster.

THE REAL THING

This is one stage of the horse's education when you must feel confident that you have both covered everything on the syllabus and that the horse will not be asked any question to which he doesn't know the answer. Like any test, the more preparation you have done beforehand, the less you have to worry about on the day. It is a lack of understanding and a fear of the unknown which will upset a horse when he is first backed, not the fact that he is carrying your weight for the first time.

To all intents and purposes, this is a normal schooling session. Work the horse in the pen to re-accustom him to the feeling of the bit and saddle, then long-rein him briefly to remind him of the lessons about stopping and turning. Make sure you have his attention, and that he is sensitive to your body language. A breastplate is always a useful additional piece of tack: it stops the saddle slipping back and so avoids upsetting the horse at a crucial moment, and it provides the rider with a neckstrap to hold on to — not because you anticipate any problems, of course, but to prevent the rider losing balance as the horse tries to find his. It is also useful to pull on the neckstrap as the horse makes a downward transition; the pressure on the trachea makes him slow down anyway and this will help him to understand what you want, with the minimum of pressure on his mouth. Reduce the chances of anything going wrong by making sure the girth is tight enough and the stirrups the right length before you start.

If the horse isn't paying attention, or things don't seem to be going particularly well for whatever reason — perhaps it is windy, or his friend is hacking out in the other direction, or you are running late — then wait for another day. Of course you are not always going to make excuses for the horse or wait for conditions to be perfect every time you ride him; as ultimately he must learn to concentrate and to do as you ask under all circumstances; but this is not the time to assert yourself, and it would be a mistake to back him out of a sense of duty and in a spirit of grim determination.

USING A HELPER

When backing a young horse, the person on the ground is more important than the person who will sit on him – and although you may have a burning desire to be the first to sit on your horse, he actually needs your help and reassurance at ground level, where he can see you. Provided that the rider is fairly lightweight, confident and balanced, it doesn't really matter whom you choose because the horse will only be conscious of the rider as an unusual weight on his back, not as an individual person.

When the horse has worked as usual with his tack on, invite him back to the centre of the circle and stay at his head while the rider prepares to mount. I sometimes have a girl rider to help me, so from now on I shall use the pronoun 'she', 'her' to describe the rider. A leg-up is the easiest way, but make sure that you and your rider have both practised beforehand – this is not the time to get it wrong and have the rider end up in a heap on the horse's back! The rider should lie on her stomach over the saddle initially, stretching a hand over to pat the horse's opposite side, and it is important to make quite a point of this, as it is the first time that he will have seen that the same human can appear on both sides of him simultaneously. Talk to him all the while to reassure him that although it seems bizarre, it is indeed a human on his back and not a horse-eating big cat!

The rider can then push herself up and over the horse's back a little further so that she can stretch forwards far enough to pat round his shoulders; it is important that the horse catches sight of the rider moving above him and on both sides. This legging up and leaning over may be repeated several times from both sides.

HOLD THE HORSE LIGHTLY

The handler should reassure the horse and talk to him constantly, but it is a mistake to keep too tight a grip on his head because this will almost certainly create anxiety and confusion in his mind, and he will start wondering what you are getting so concerned about! He will (rightly) translate such restriction as 'This is a lot to ask, and I'm worried you'll get in a panic', whereas the message you need to convey to him is, 'This is

nothing you should mind about, there is no reason for you to be in the least alarmed.'

Holding on to the horse too tightly also goes against the basic principle of your relationship, which is that he is free to react naturally and to make his own decisions. By putting a rider on his back and telling him it's nothing to worry about, you are asking the biggest favour yet, and you rely totally on the horse's co-operation. However, there is no reason why he shouldn't believe you and go along with it quite happily – although he is less likely to if he feels bullied. If he feels you are threatening him, at this or at any other stage, your relationship could risk turning into a trial of strength which you can only lose.

SITTING UP

The most frightening moment for the horse is when he sees a rider appear on a level with his head for the first time, looming over his withers in the same way as a predator would in the wild. His first experience of this was when the rider leaned over him and pushed herself above the level of his ears earlier, patting his opposite shoulder.

When he appears to have accepted this, the rider can swing her leg over his hindquarters, being careful not to touch them as she does so, and sit astride the horse, keeping most of her weight off his back and her upper body low. The handler should be a good enough judge of the horse's expressions and body language to tell whether or not he is happy to continue; if he is, the rider can gradually drop more weight onto the saddle and work herself slowly into an upright position, talking to the horse all the time and stroking his neck and shoulder on both sides.

When the rider is sitting upright in a normal riding position she should stay there for a few minutes; then dismount and do it all over again, until the horse is used to her mounting and dismounting. The rider should never try to be subtle by sliding on and off quietly – whatever you do should be positive and obvious so the horse knows exactly what is going on and learns to tolerate it with increasing confidence. He may in fact be more alarmed by the rider dismounting; although this might seem to be the easiest stage, he will be very conscious of the weight suddenly disappearing from his back.

MOVING OFF

Horses are generally happy to stand still with a dead weight on their backs, but they often find it difficult to adjust their balance when they try to move off;

▶ Despite your apprehension don't be over-cautious when mounting a youngster for the first time. He will feed off your confidence

▼ Try to spread your weight as evenly as possible over the horse's back and when the horse first starts to move, imagine you are just another piece of equipment. Lie still!

◀ When the horse accepts your presence on his back happily, swing your leg over his quarters purposefully and quietly. Keep your head and upper body low on his neck initially

▼ Get your foot in the stirrup as soon as possible to ensure you stay balanced. Have a quiet but experienced handler to help

▶ On the move. The handler should initiate forward movement

▼ As the horse gains confidence, the rider can start using subtle leg and rein aids. The handler must resist the urge to step in and 'help out' if horse and rider seem to be running into difficulty, because the horse needs to concentrate on what the rider is telling him – he should not keep looking to the handler and expecting him to make life easy for him again

however good the rider is, she is bound to have a very unbalancing effect on the horse – it might be equated to carrying a badly packed rucksack which wobbles around on your back! Nevertheless, this is the next 'hurdle', so once the rider is sitting comfortably upright, the handler should lead the horse forwards for a few steps so he can experience the loss of balance which moving entails. The rider should not have any contact on the reins yet – the handler is in charge of speed and steering – and she must be aware that the horse will be quite unpredictable – he may get 'stuck' in halt and then lurch forwards, for instance – so she should keep her weight slightly forward and slip a hand through the neckstrap to prevent her losing her own balance or getting left behind.

GOING SOLO

The handler should be controlling the stopping and starting practice initially, but once the horse gets the idea, the rider can pick up the reins on a loose contact and use gentle rein and leg aids, timing them to coincide with the handler's instructions to the horse. Use the aids as little as

▲ Dismounting is as important as mounting, and can be as much of a shock to the horse on the first occasion as getting on him

▶ Note how the handler has a hand on the horse's neck throughout, in order to steady him

possible, but as much as necessary; as a rule this means a lot of leg and very little hand – or none at all – to get any result. The handler can then gradually drop back and allow the rider more control, until it seems safe to remove the lead-rope. Horse and rider are now going solo! Taking signals from someone on his back will seem very strange to the horse, but as a result of his long-reining lessons and all his other preparatory work, he should have a basic understanding of what is being asked.

TIPS FOR THE RIDER

Keep it very simple at this stage and don't be tempted to over-ride: the horse is learning a foreign language, and just a few simple but useful words of vocabulary are all that is needed – basically leg means go, hand means slow. Trying to ride perfectly, and worrying that you will 'spoil' the youngster if you don't, will not benefit anybody – he won't have a clue about the subtleties of equestrianism at this stage, so relax and try to be effective rather than worrying about what you look like. This is between you and the horse, so ignore the handler and anything else which is going on, and concentrate on communicating with him.

Turning and changing direction will take quite a while to perfect, so use a very obvious, open rein to guide the horse, being careful not to pull backwards even slightly. Vocal commands will help the horse understand what you are asking for. When you want to stop, pulling back on a neckstrap at the same time as you gently pull on the reins takes the pressure off the horse's mouth and helps him to understand the command.

Rather than carrying a whip to back up your leg aids, try flicking the end of the reins over the withers from one of the horse's shoulders to the other to get him moving forwards, or carry a soft piece of rope to tickle him behind your leg. These methods will regain his attention in a way that the whip never does, the effect being more of irritation than actually being hit.

Start as you mean to go on, and be careful not to make life too easy for the horse. He has to learn to think for himself, so ride him past spooky areas and make him walk over poles and up and down banks, because if you don't, you may give him the idea that he can avoid them, and he may not take kindly to you changing the rules in a few weeks' time when you decide he is ready to face them!

Once the horse has learned the basic aids for stopping, starting and turning, dismount and then mount again by yourself before you finish the lesson. It is good for him to realise that if you get off his back, this does not always mean the end of the training session.

DUMMY RIDERS

An old-fashioned way to avoid getting on an unbacked horse is to stuff a straw dummy and attach it to the saddle, the idea being that if the horse bucks and plunges, the rider won't come off in the way a human might. If the rider needs to see this to give them the confidence to back the horse, then they are not up to the job.

There is absolutely no benefit in using a dummy rider to back a young horse. Not only does it feel entirely different to carrying a live rider for the horse, it is extremely difficult to attach securely and can cause irreversible mental and possibly physical damage if it

▶ Horses do not necessarily follow their noses! Steering takes time to perfect. Remember that youngsters find balancing with a rider difficult and will not always react as you expect

▼ (Below left) Don't stifle the horse's movement – a strong contact can cause panic

▼ (Below right) When he is used to carrying the rider, the horse must learn to do two things at once. Pole work is excellent for improving his co-ordination

▲ Don't 'cry wolf' with your 'stop' aid by holding on to a young horse's head

slips under the horse and between his back legs. While it is not desirable for a human rider to fall off, it is preferable for this to happen than for a dummy not to come off if things go wrong, causing the horse to panic.

Dummy riders are occasionally used in expert hands for older horses with severe ridden problems as a last resort, but are in no way necessary for any young horse about to be backed.

REFUSING TO MOVE

People are often surprised to find that, far from being hypersensitive and forward-going, and liable to bolt off at any minute, young horses can be rather sluggish, and are generally slow to move away from the leg because they have no idea what a leg aid really means. They are also struggling to control their limbs and find their balance. Just as you learn a new dance routine by going through the steps slowly, correcting mistakes and only speeding up gradually, so must the horse be given time to learn co-ordination.

A young horse which refuses to move forwards and gets 'stuck' in a corner of the school or in front of a ground pole, is a very common problem. However, far from being a sign of a reluctant, nappy horse, it is more a case of the horse standing there thinking 'Oh my goodness, I've forgotten how to do it. Somebody, *help*!'

Usually if you can persuade him to take just one step in any direction, he will then initiate the following movement and so will continue quite happily. Flicking the reins from shoulder to shoulder or slapping his side with a soft piece of rope is very effective, especially when combined with opening one rein and asking for a sideways step rather than a forward one.

The other thing which makes horses freeze and refuse to go forward, or to stop and explode, is severe

back or neck pain, in which case trying to force him to continue is cruel and counter-productive. Have his back, teeth and tack checked by an expert, and don't stop looking until you have found the root of the problem.

▲ Young horses are often reluctant to go forwards. A short piece of rope flicked behind the leg or the reins flicked from one shoulder to the other can be more effective in teaching a horse to go forwards than a hefty kick in the ribs

RIDING AWAY

Walking is comparatively easy, so don't allow the horse to rest in that comfort zone for too long before asking him to trot and canter. To ask for an upward transition, let go of his head and use your legs and voice to ask for just a few strides at a time. This is simply to get him used to the feel of it, so don't be too particular about having the correct diagonal or canter lead. Be logical and ask for upward transitions towards the gate, and downward transitions away from it — it makes sense to use anything which makes your life easier and helps the horse to understand what you are asking for.

Horses are often more balanced in canter than in trot, as this is the pace they use most in the wild, so use that knowledge to your advantage; they spend very little time in trot. When you are ready to canter it may seem sensible to stay in the school, but cantering a small circle is hard work for any horse, never mind a youngster. Choosing a wide open space will make it easier for you both, as it will seem natural to the horse, to *offer* canter in such a situation. Keep a light seat, although don't sit too far forward in case the horse bucks or stumbles — there is nothing more frightening for him at this stage than you falling off! It is unusual for a horse to be naughty at this stage, he has far too many other things to think about!

▲ Establish the horse's basic obedience and paces in the school before venturing out

LOOKING FORWARD

A good relationship with your horse is central to the success of the breaking and riding process. Also, it is essential that his training is progressive and that he is given time to understand and adjust to each new demand you make before you move on to the next stage. Keep each session short and interesting so that the horse looks back on being ridden as a positive experience. Stay in the school until you can start, stop, change pace and turn comfortably – this will not

necessarily be in perfect style! – before introducing him to the sights and sounds of the big world outside.

As you will see from the next chapter, I believe that young horses should venture out alone for their first few rides, rather than relying on a schoolmaster to be brave for them. By now the horse should see you as his constant source of help and comfort in the midst of new experiences, and if he believes in you, he will do what you want without question. If you get into difficulties he should see you as the comfort zone, just as he did in the early days when you joined up and worked him in the pen. Your role in the relationship is strongest the very first time you ask him to do something new, not several weeks later when he has worked it out for himself.

If you misjudge a situation and things do go wrong, take a step back onto familiar territory to regain the horse's confidence before re-introducing the new idea. Take each day as it comes, and don't become obsessed with the end result of actually riding the horse. A fully broken horse is the result of years of correct training, introducing one new step at a time, and sitting on him is just one of these small steps. Backing the horse is a means to an end, not an end in itself.

▶ Panic or over-excitement are generally quickly overcome if you have spent time establishing the groundwork in the school

STAGE 8
CHECKPOINTS

- ■ Judge when to back by your horse's attitude, not just by his age.
- ■ Everything connected with the backing procedure should already be familiar to the horse – the time, place, tack and people.
- ■ Careful preparation is the best way to build confidence in horse and rider.
- ■ Don't hang on to the horse as if you expect things to go wrong.
- ■ The rider's stirrups should be a little shorter than usual to help keep a light, balanced seat.
- ■ Use a breastplate to stop the saddle slipping.
- ■ Leave taking up a rein contact until last.
- ■ The 'softly, softly' approach is not a confidence-giver. Positive action is appreciated by a young horse.
- ■ Keep it simple: leg means go, hand means slow.
- ■ Aim to ride effectively, and don't worry what it looks like. It's impossible to ride beautifully on a horse which has just been backed!
- ■ When using the aids, ask as little as possible, but as much and as often as necessary.
- ■ Don't panic if the horse gets 'stuck' – flick him with the end of the reins and ask him to take a sideways rather than a forward step to help make him move.
- ■ Keep the session short – however willing he is, the horse has not developed strong back muscles yet and even a light human will feel very heavy.
- ■ Aim to complete the whole backing procedure in one session.

STAGE 9
HACKING HAZARDS
Age: 3–5 years

So the moment has come. After all this preparation you are finally on board your youngster. You can walk, trot, canter and change direction reasonably well, and you know you can't stay in the school forever! Although it feels as if you have both come a long way, this is actually just the beginning of the horse's career. By now you may be longing for the time when your horse is more experienced and able to teach *you* a thing or two, but for the moment, it is up to you to continue his education. He still has so much to learn.

GO IT ALONE

Opinion is divided as to the best way to introduce a young horse to the various hazards of the big outside world, and what to do when you meet the unexpected. Many people think it helps the youngster if he is allowed to follow an older horse for a while, but I am completely against this idea. Contrary to popular belief, horses seem to learn very little from watching others. If it were that simple, all we would need to do is to set up stables round an arena and work a dressage horse and a show jumper in there, to teach them everything they need to know!

Very often, riding out with an older horse is an emotional crutch for the rider rather than the youngster. In my experience it doesn't actually work that well either – I've never found that having an older horse there will stop a young horse bolting or misbehaving if he wants to.

Of all the difficult horses which have made their way to my yard, I have never had one which won't go

out with others! However, nappiness and refusing to go out alone are very common, and are often caused by a horse being in the habit of following somebody else. Be aware of this tendency in a herd animal like the horse, and avoid creating a potential problem. A young horse may come to resent going out on his own not because he lacks boldness, but simply because he is used to following someone else – so don't give him the chance to learn bad habits.

Examine your own motives for wanting another horse to go first: is it really to boost the horse's confidence, or is it the rider who needs reassuring? If you aren't brave enough to go it alone, perhaps you are not the right person to be guiding a young horse through his first experiences of life.

TAKE THE LEAD

When a young horse needs help to deal with a new experience, he should take his lead from the rider, not another horse. If your youngster does need reassurance, then the only person he should seek it from is you. You have placed yourself at the top of the herd hierarchy, and you will confuse the delicate issue of who is boss if you suddenly rely on someone else to take the lead.

Some horses are more independent than others, so when deciding what they are capable of, you must assess each horse as an individual. Establish in your mind that everything must take as long as it needs to. There is no hurry, no deadline, no schedule. Take each day as it comes and let the horse dictate the pace. Remember that every ridden experience should be a pleasant one, and that the youngster will still be physically incapable of carrying a rider very far.

▲ Don't 'nanny' your youngster! This horse enters the school a slightly different way – a small hazard in its own right

▶ Rather than trying to avoid places where you think you might meet more alarming hazards, you should go out of your way to encounter them. The young horse should be taken out on his own from the very start. If he believes in you and has been properly prepared and is competently ridden, this should not be a problem. Make it a very short trip at first, literally just a few hundred yards around the yard, and increase the distance as the horse's confidence grows – though be careful not to demand too much, too soon

LEARNING TO COPE WITH HAZARDS

There has to be a first time for you and your young horse to come face to face with that lorry or combine harvester! It really is a case of the earlier the better, because the less confident and footsure the horse is, the less likely he is to try and play up or be nappy. You will not do your youngster any favours by trying to protect him from the realities of life: on the contrary, it is better to prepare him right from the start, rather than be caught out at a later date.

It is up to you to stay as relaxed and confident as possible as you approach any hazards. Remember that an over-cautious approach will sap the horse's confidence, so take care not to send out subconscious warning signs that you are expecting trouble, such as shortening your reins or gripping with your legs. After all the preparation you have put in on the ground, your horse should be responsive to the voice by now, so use this to your advantage.

If the horse stops going forwards and gets 'stuck' as you get closer to the hazard, flick a short piece of rope or the end of the reins from shoulder to shoulder. I find this much more effective than a whip, which in any case only works on one side of the horse and is too easy to abuse.

IN TIMES OF PANIC

So what happens if things do go wrong and your young horse gets a fright on a hack? The answer is to sit tight in order to help him maintain his balance and co-ordination as far as is possible. Grabbing at the reins and losing your own balance is likely to panic him even more, so keep your stirrups fairly short and use a neckstrap until the horse is more predictable.

It is at times like this that all the work you have done on the ground – persuading the horse to trust

you and breaking down his flight instinct – will prove worthwhile. In my experience, few youngsters run very far if they do shy – they just don't have the strength and the balance to do so. This is also the case if the horse gets strong and excited when you canter in the open, for example.

USE A VARIED PROGRAMME

The more balanced and confident the youngster becomes with you on his back, the more likely he is to be naughty, so don't wait too long before moving on to something new: occupy his mind before he thinks of something by himself. However, remember that educating a young horse requires just enough work to stimulate his mind without straining his body – more problems are caused by missing the mark in either direction.

Schooling doesn't have to entail endless circles. Introduce poles to improve your horse's co-ordination and to add interest.

Raised poles will be his first introduction to jumping, and you can work him loose or on a lunge over small fences to give him the idea without the encumbrance of a rider.

◀ Effective riding is necessary when taking out a youngster, even if it doesn't look very stylish! Your natural instinct may be to shorten the rein as you pass a hazard, but in fact the opposite is needed, and it is better to slacken them

▶ Be versatile with poles: don't just go over trotting poles again and again – make him pick his way through fans, stars, parallel poles and 'L' shapes

◀ The first canter. Make sure you have plenty of space, and then let him go – he will run out of steam long before you do, and realise that galloping about is pretty hard work!

THE FIRST SHOW

STAGE 9
CHECKPOINTS

- Take the young horse out on his own right from the start, to discourage nappiness.

- Flick the horse across the shoulders with a rope or the end of the reins to encourage him to move forwards.

- Don't avoid hazards or keep making excuses for the young horse, but go out of your way to find new things.

- Remember, the emphasis is on mental stimulation, not physical exertion.

- Positive riding is more important than a perfect position! The horse will gain confidence from you.

- Look for signs of boredom, and move on to something more challenging before the horse has a chance to get cocky.

- Keep your schooling imaginative.

- Take each day as it comes, and let the horse dictate the pace.

- A show is not the time or the place to school a youngster.

- The horse must enjoy being ridden, so make every experience positive.

Once you have hacked about a bit, why not go to a small show? You don't actually have to compete – just go for the ride and to soak up the atmosphere, or do a basic dressage test or small jumping class. As ever, preparation is the key to success, so make sure you have done your homework. The horse should be used to wearing boots and a tail bandage, and also to travelling.

If the horse is properly halter-broken you should have no trouble loading, but do practise several times

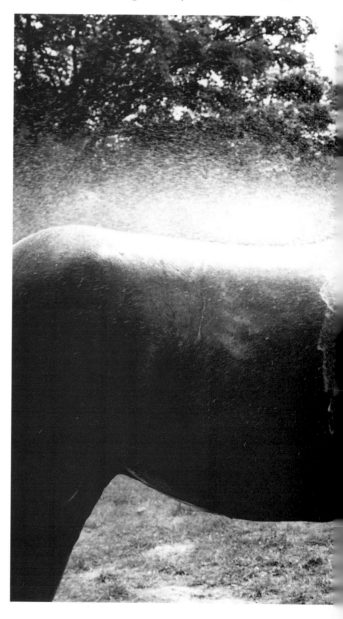

▶ Allow plenty of time to finish everything you start because stable management jobs will take much longer with a fidgety youngster – tasks such as plaiting, or washing his tail or hosing him down may all be unfamiliar, so already this simple outing is turning into a big learning experience

before the big day. Coming out of a horsebox can be as big a problem as going in for a youngster – the slope of the ramp can seem quite intimidating from the top, and requires more bravery and balance than walking up!

As well as making the whole outing more pleasant for both horse and handler, the preparation you do at home is also a safety issue in that a youngster could cause havoc if he decides to play up and get away from you. All your training will be put to the test in the exciting show atmosphere, and it may highlight a few weak links; but the showground is not the place to school any horse, never mind an inexperienced youngster. Use the day to learn from your mistakes and those of the horse, and use them as a basis for future schooling at home.

As well as being excited by all the showground distractions, your youngster may be quite intimidated by the number of other horses and the general show atmosphere – but remember, he will draw confidence from disciplined, familiar handling. However, if you really want to put your training to the test, then hand him over to a friend for a while. A change of handler should make no difference to his behaviour if his lessons have been really well learned: he should know exactly what sort of behaviour is expected and where his boundaries are under all circumstances, and with all handlers.

Good behaviour also leaves you and the horse free to concentrate on performance, and the day will be remembered as an enjoyable and valuable learning experience, rather than as a battle.

STARTS

All Ages

Just because a horse is young does not automatically mean he is going to be difficult to handle in day-to-day life, provided he is fairly and consistently handled from birth. The emphasis of this book is on the prevention of problems rather than their cure; however, we all make mistakes, and provided that you recognise where you have gone wrong, and as long as you apologise and backtrack immediately, the horse is usually quite forgiving. Luckily for us it is very rare to find a real rogue in the horse world, although every horse has its own temper and tolerance level, and this must be respected – like humans, some horses are more volatile and short-tempered than others!

Problems also arise when people take on a horse that is sharper than they anticipated, or too advanced for their ability, or one where the groundwork has not been done by previous owners. Don't dismiss a straightforward character clash, either – I have seen many cases where horse and handler simply don't get on, and have been well advised to go their separate ways before resentment and a loss of confidence occurs on either side.

Whilst it is easier on both horse and human if we get things right from the start, it is rarely too late to correct any lapses in behaviour – so don't panic if things are not going according to plan. Rather, look on the situation as a chance to further your relationship with the horse by helping him come to terms with whatever is bothering him. Horses are not unco-operative or confrontational by nature – quite the opposite, in fact – and just about every behavioural problem can be tackled successfully if you are 100 per cent committed to breaking the behaviour pattern. As I have explained in preceding chapters, our great advantage when training the horse is that he is a naturally subservient creature that responds to reason and logic. In fact, his logical mind can be the very reason that he develops behavioural problems in the first place! Bad behaviour often starts as a highly intelligent and reasonable reaction towards something the horse perceives as a threat, based on his natural survival instincts. If a horse can run from danger then he always will, but if he is cornered and forced to face that danger, then he will consider that he has no choice but to fight: his survival instincts dictate that he must kick, bite, rear, bolt or barge his way out of trouble, so this is what he does.

PROBLEM HORSE OR PROBLEM OWNER?

There is always a good reason why a horse feels he cannot do what is being asked of him, so if he suddenly starts exhibiting signs of 'problem' behaviour, sit down and ask yourself *why* before it escalates out of control.

Take, for example, the horse that is nappy and refuses to hack out or to leave the yard alone. Why would a normally placid flight animal who trusts his rider, understands what he has to do and is physically capable of doing it, suddenly decide to stand up and fight, refusing to do as he is asked? The answer is, he wouldn't, under normal circumstances. But what if he does *not* trust his rider, does *not* understand what he has to do, or is *not* physically capable of doing it? In this case maybe he feels justified in napping, in an attempt to make *us* understand *his* message — he can't speak our language, but in his way he's shouting as loudly as he can.

And what do we usually do in response to this cry for help? All too often we push the horse harder, 'show him who's boss' and make him do even more of whatever it is which is causing him pain or anxiety.

The thinking behind 'show him who's boss' is that, because a horse is physically bigger and stronger than a human, if you give an inch he might take a mile. The fact is, that if a horse wants to, he's perfectly capable of taking a mile, whatever you do! Being severe to stop your horse 'trying it on' is rather like smacking a child just in case it decides to be naughty. In fact it is far better to wait until the child has actually misbehaved and *then* correct him with an immediate and appropriate remonstrance, so that he associates the punishment with the crime.

Look at it from the horse's point of view. If someone marches up to you, pokes you in the chest

◀▲ The horse must trust and respect you before you can solve any problems

and shouts at you, you are understandably reluctant to do what that person wants. A polite and reasonable request from a friend is an entirely different matter, however, and has a much higher success rate than the first option! Think of this as you deal with your horse. Use mental tactics to assert your authority, because in the long term, physical domination just cannot work with horses.

AVOID VIOLENCE

The key to problem-solving is to react immediately, with firmness and confidence, and never to use force or violence against the horse, however frustrating the situation may be. If you do, it will assuredly be only a matter of time before the horse realises that he is stronger than you, and then your roles will reverse – he

becomes boss, and you really *are* on the slippery slope! With a problem horse you do have to be utterly determined to get your way and to see things through, but you should never become violent: if you do, then the horse has every right to feel hard done by, he will trust the rider even less, his confusion will increase, and any physical discomfort he feels will get even worse as he is forced to perform. By this time, needless to say, both horse and rider are caught in a vicious circle.

Handling a horse that is testing your authority is like dealing with a child who howls and sobs himself to sleep because he is not allowed to watch his favourite TV programme. Ignore the hysteria, quietly insist that the child does as he is told, and next time he won't even bother asking. The worst thing you can do is to back down and let him watch TV after a fight. You may gain temporary peace for the time being, but you have lost his respect and have set up a potentially hazardous scenario for next time because you have taught him that 'no' sometimes means 'yes', and that he can control you with bad behaviour. Horses play this game too!

Never be tempted to gang up on a horse, either; only insecure people feel the need to tackle a problem with their gang behind them, and 'one to one' is far more decisive when it comes to settling arguments than the 'school bully' approach. This will only cause the horse to become defensive and so even less likely to co-operate — if he feels threatened, he will 'fight his corner'.

Bribing with food is also futile because it is avoiding the issue rather than solving it — and like the schoolboy who tries to buy friends, you will only be popular until the sweeties run out.

CAUSE OR SYMPTOM?

The key to effective problem-solving is to find out and eliminate the *cause* of the problem, not just to tackle the symptom. If you are a sympathetic, thinking rider, you will realise that you don't have to risk your neck trying to ride 'dangerous' horses 'through a problem' — in other words, it's all very well sitting tight and hitting a nappy horse until it goes where you want it to, but this only tackles the symptom, when the actual *cause* of the problem might be a sore back or sharp teeth: these cause the horse to associate work with pain, a scenario which will not be resolved by strong riding. In fact strong riding will make matters worse because it will compound the horse's discomfort and confirm in his mind that he is absolutely right *not* to co-operate.

THE PAIN FACTOR

Over 99 per cent of the problem horses I see, many of which have come to me as a last resort after becoming positively dangerous to ride and handle, have some kind of physiological problem that has forced them to behave in an extreme manner in order to make themselves heard. They may well have started off just making a grumpy face or swishing their tail, but when their

handler ignored these gentle hints that they were not happy, they were forced to take more drastic measures, and a head-on battle resulted. A horse in pain can behave recklessly, and no matter how experienced you are, such battles are unnerving. At best you will stop enjoying your horse and at worst you will be seriously hurt.

A horse does not understand pain in the same way as you or I do, or reason about what is causing it. Neither can they alter their work load accordingly — for this, they rely on you. It is your responsibility to take action on their behalf, and to ensure that the horse is kept as happy and as comfortable as possible until the problem is sorted out. Horses are not hypochondriacs — if they say something hurts, you have to believe them even if you can't see the cause immediately. Like humans, horses also have different levels of tolerance to pain. Some will make a tremendous fuss over a tweaked muscle and hop around looking sorry for themselves, while others soldier on bravely ignoring considerable levels of pain for as long as they can. It is a question of knowing what is normal for your horse and handling it accordingly.

▼ Good management plays an important part in ensuring the horse gives his best, without resentment. These hooves need the attention of a farrier, before they split and cause pain

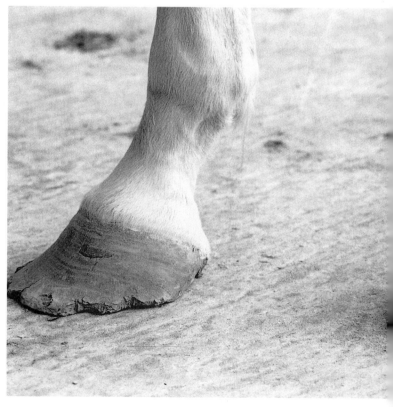

Ironically it can be the most honest, willing horses that are the worst cases, because their desire to please overrides their need to complain. Such horses can suffer in silence for years before they are physically unable to take any more, and because their memory of pain is so long-standing, it can take much longer for them to forgive and forget when they arrive in my yard.

IS MY HORSE IN PAIN?

Listed below are some of the most typical signs of a horse in pain or discomfort. Sadly, many of these are seen on a daily basis at many yards, and are ignored.

- Observe your horse when he is loose: does he move freely and happily, appear interested in his surroundings, and graze more or less continuously? Can he get up and down to roll with ease on both sides, or does he only ever roll on one side? Does he canter round the field on both leads and do flying changes when he changes direction? If the answer to any of these questions is no, your horse may be in some discomfort even without the weight of a rider.
- In the stable, does your horse turn his quarters to you or move to the back of the stable when you enter? Does he make faces or swish his tail when you approach with tack or alter his rugs? Does he fidget when being groomed? Is he reluctant to open his mouth for the bit? Does he shake his head even when there are no flies about? The answers should be no.
- When you come to ride him, does your horse try and move away as you mount? Does he chew the bit excessively, or not at all? Does he tip his head to one side? Is he worse on one rein, or does he find certain canter leads difficult? Does he buck, rush his fences or sometimes refuse? Is he nappy about leaving the stable or yard? If the answer to any of these questions is yes, your horse may have a problem related to tooth or back pain.

TEETH AND BACKS

I don't even attempt to start work on a so-called 'problem' horse until both a good chiropractor and a specialist equine dentist have seen to them. Often after treatment there is obvious relief to be seen in the

▼ Andy Andrews checks for tension, which may result in poor communication and lack of co-operation between horse and rider if left untreated

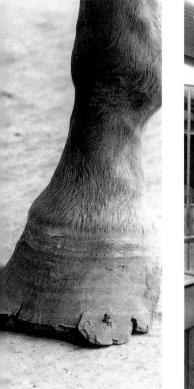

horse's expression, and very often its behaviour will change overnight. It must be said that there are a lot of 'teeth and back men' out there who see countless horses, but who come nowhere near to solving their problems. Unfortunately, owners will then often tick the 'pain' option off their list of possible causes of bad behaviour or loss of performance, assuming – quite rightly – that the so-called 'expert' has sorted things out. Every concerned owner who sends me a problem horse assures me that they have had the animal's teeth and back checked – yet by whom? The specialists I work with, Andy Andrews and Robin Abel-Smith, are usually horrified by what they find in horses that have supposedly been treated.

This is a difficult situation, and I pity not just the horses but also the owners, who genuinely believe that they have done everything they can for their animals. I don't know what the answer is, because at the moment there are simply not enough bona fide specialists to outnumber the cowboys; however, there are certain points that can guide your choice. For instance, an equine dentist should arrive at your yard with a good selection of clean rasps and cutters, not just one; he should always use a gag to keep the horse's mouth open, and he should allow you to feel the horse's teeth before and after treatment, explaining any potential problem areas fully; finally he should be interested in any comments you have on the horse's eating habits, on its acceptance – or not – of the bit, or regarding its head carriage when ridden. Wolf teeth and hooks should be removed, and the dentist should work right to the back of the horse's mouth. He should take his time and charge a reasonable fee for the service – if he is very cheap, then be suspicious! Most horses, apart from the very young or very old, will only need their teeth seeing to once a year if it is done properly.

Assessing an equine physiotherapist or chiropractor is more difficult, but they too should be interested in the whole horse – his diet, foot balance, tack, way of going and so on – rather than just focusing on what appears to be the site of the problem. In my experience the problem area is rarely under the saddle as this is an extremely strong part of the horse's back, where the spine is protected by deep layers of muscle; for the same reason, no amount of prodding and slapping by a physiotherapist is going to push it back into alignment. Even though the horse's way of going often appears to point to the saddle area, the source of the problem is more often found in the neck or pelvis which then translates back to the saddle area under the weight of a rider.

The horse doesn't have to have a terrible fall or accident to damage the neck or pelvis. Slipping in the field, tripping, rough games with other horses or simply rolling and getting up awkwardly are sufficient to cause a niggling pain which, if left untreated, can cause considerable discomfort as the horse stiffens against it and seeks to compensate for it when being worked. You may find the horse appears much stiffer on one rein, starts cantering disunited or prefers one canter lead over the other; at the other extreme a horse in pain will refuse or rush fences, buck, rear or nap. There is more to solving this sort of behaviour than correct schooling.

Depending on the type of problem, you may also have to look further than the actual horse for the source of his discomfort – but I assure you that if you look hard enough, you will find your answer somewhere. If a horse won't load for example, is it because he has a rough ride or feels claustrophobic in a horsebox? If he rips his rugs off, is it because he is simply too hot? Finally, let your horse be the judge as to whether he hurts or not, and always give him the benefit of the doubt. No matter how many people have checked his back and teeth, if he says he is sore and unhappy, he is certainly not making it up!

READY TO RIDE

Once you have truly eliminated any physical discomfort, then you can set about changing history! It is not just the pain you had to get rid of, it is the memory of that pain and the horse's habit of reacting to it that must be overcome. If you have had an injury that has caused you to sit crookedly for several weeks, you will continue to sit crookedly even when the injury has healed, firstly through habit and secondly because the associated muscle you will have developed unevenly as a result of compensating for the injury. Bear this in mind as you rehabilitate your problem horse, and remember that the longer he has had the problem, the longer it will take him to get over it. You may have to settle for making the problem manageable rather than eliminating it altogether.

If your own confidence has taken a knock because of a particular horse's behaviour, then understandably, you may not want to get back on until you know you can trust the horse again. Calm confidence, and not

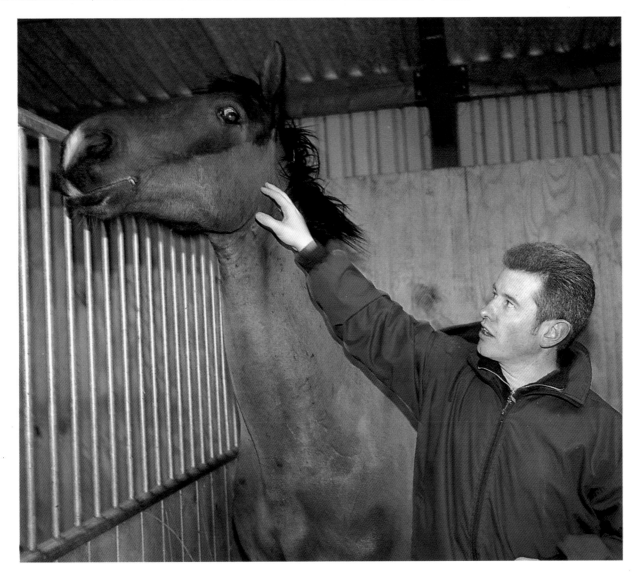

▲ Is this horse headshy, or is he just being evasive? It is important to know the difference so that you can handle the situation accordingly

CONFRONTING FEAR

heroics, solves behavioural problems, so if you are not 100 per cent confident and committed to seeing things through, then ask another competent rider or handler to take over for a while – this should *not* be seen as a personal failure, it is just good sense, and is fairer on you and the horse. You can kid yourself that you are ready, but you'll never kid the horse! Horses are notoriously good at interpreting their handler's state of mind, and there is certainly no room for doubt when you are dealing with remedial cases. You can get involved again at a later stage, but if you want a horse to believe that you have the ability to cure its problem, then you must believe it yourself.

The problems which people can experience with their horses, both ridden and in hand, are endless, but the principle behind treating them remains the same: remove any physical discomfort, then re-establish mutual trust and respect. The horse must realise that while you are a friend and will not seek to dominate him by force, you still hold the casting vote when you both meet at the negotiating table.

Work on achieving good 'join-up' with the horse (see Stage 4) and make sure that he has retained his respect for your personal space by sharpening up his response to the halter (as in Stage 4). When it comes to asking significant questions of the horse, be careful to

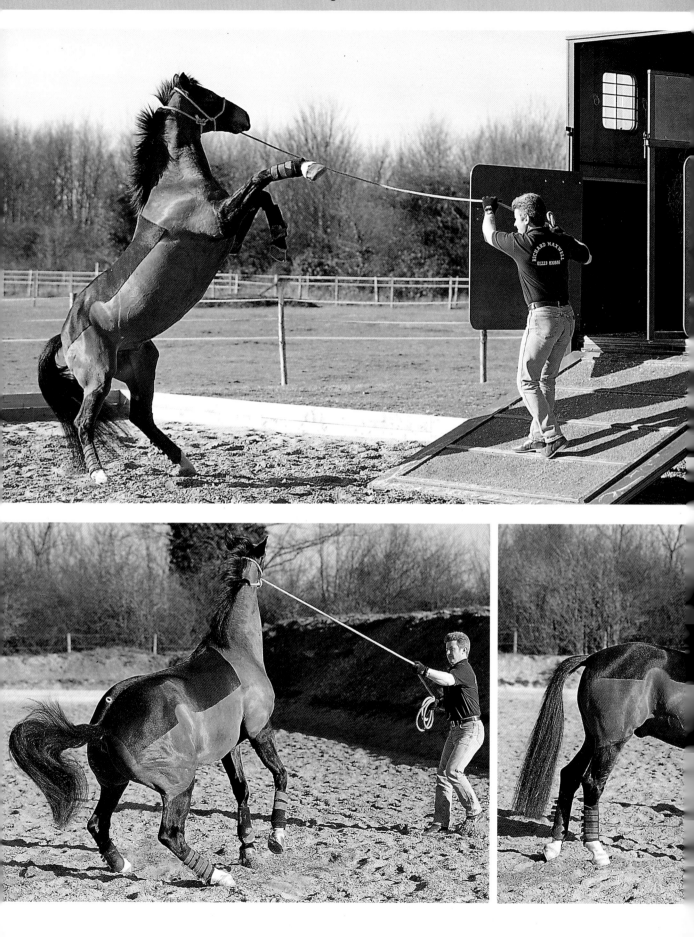

do so politely – your attitude must always be 'please will you', not 'you must', when you ask him to do something. Ask courteously and you have a better chance of getting a courteous reply.

There is a very good reason why the problem horse facing rehabilitation must trust and respect his handler: you are shortly going to ask him to confront his fear by putting him into the very situation that he dreads, and he will only be prepared to be brave and give it a go if he feels you are his ally. For example, if he is reluctant to load into a horsebox, this is exactly what you must both do, time and time again, until the horse realises that it really is nothing to worry about. In fact, because you are there telling him he is clever and you are the friend he seeks to please, he may even start to enjoy it!

◀ Whatever reasons this horse has for not going into the lorry, he is only going to overcome them by getting in there and realising that it's not as bad as he thought

▼ (Below left and centre) I take him away from the site of the problem – the lorry – and remind him that he must respect and respond to the slightest pressure on the halter. Soon he is shadowing my movements as he should, and carefully maintaining the slack in the lead-rope of his own accord
▼ (Below right) This lesson is put to the test a while later as we approach the lorry ramp; as far as the horse is concerned the same rules apply, and he responds to the pressure on his halter and loads easily. A few minutes later, this horse followed me up the ramp and loaded without wearing a halter at all

Begin by reschooling the horse away from the problem area. For the problem loader, this means making him shadow your every move, becoming so respectful of the halter that he follows you even without a rope. For the nappy horse, it means making him highly responsive to the leg, and being quite sure that he understands the aids to go forward beyond a shadow of a doubt before you ask him to go out of the yard, and so on.

THE FINAL FRONTIER

Once you have done your homework, the horse must be placed in the very situation he finds difficult – he must be made to confront his fear. Only by going into the lorry, or out of the yard on his own, will he realise that he can do it and that it doesn't hurt, until new habits gradually supersede the old. Imagine your own feelings when you confront an old fear or anxiety, such as diving off that high board for the first time as a child, standing up and making a speech in front of people, finding your way around a foreign city alone, getting rid of a huge spider in the bath… Once you have faced your fear and survived, you are not only relieved, but elated, proud, satisfied – and often looking forward to doing it again as soon as possible! The horse experiences similar feelings, and the bond he has with you, the friend who helped him through his fear, will increase correspondingly.

TOUGH TACTICS

If you are sure that the horse has understood exactly what is required, and has every reason to trust you yet still won't co-operate, then you have the right to get a little tough at this stage. I have come across horses whose habits are so ingrained that they will no longer play the game, and it takes drastic action to put them back on track. You have to be harder on this type of horse and make him responsible for his own actions. If he throws a temper tantrum when he is asked to do something, then he is the one creating an unpleasant situation and so let him punish himself – stand back and let him get on with it before asking again. *Always* ask nicely, even if you aren't getting very polite answers back! Think of an hysterical child – smacking him will make matters worse, and giving in rewards bad behaviour; but if you are patient enough to leave him until he has cried himself out alone, you will have a much more subdued and co-operative individual to deal with.

I have often experienced this with horses that are determined non-loaders. They will strike out at me, spin, rear and even lie down at the bottom of the ramp rather than go up it and lose face. To see this sort of behaviour through to the very end is tough on the handler and it can take hours, and is very intimidating. The only comfort you have is knowing that the worse the horse's behaviour gets, the closer he is to giving in once and for all. It is a kind of grand finale, taking you to the very edge to test your worthiness as team leader.

Tough tactics require good judgement, patience and total confidence in order not to make things worse and send the horse back a step. You don't have to be an expert, you just have to know your horse and interpret what he's trying to tell you.

REHABILITATING THE OWNER

It is not just the horses who need to confront their fear in order to overcome a problem, it's the owners too! After I have spent time rehabilitating a problem horse, I insist that the owner comes to spend time with their animal at my yard until their confidence returns and they can do everything without my help. This is not easy for them, because before sending a problem horse to me, owners have often had a terrible time trying to cope alone, and this has usually sapped their

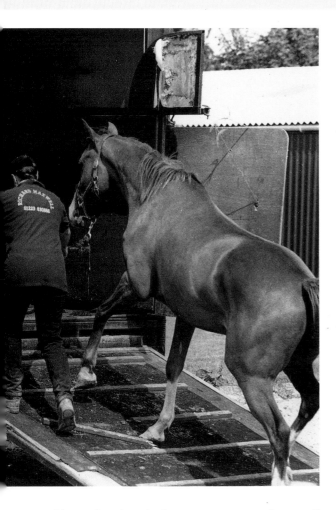

This horse is responsible for his own discomfort as he fights the pressure halter. After an hour's patient schooling in the pressure halter, he loads willingly in an ordinary headcollar

STAGE 10
CHECKPOINTS

- Never beat, bribe or beg a horse to co-operate. Logical handling is much more effective.

- Suspect pain if a horse is being unco-operative or aggressive. It is not in his nature to be so.

- Be honest about your own ability before you take on a problem horse.

- The horse will forgive you small mistakes if you apologise immediately. Taking a temporary backward step in his training will help regain his confidence.

- Be 100 per cent committed to breaking negative behaviour patterns in the horse when you take him on – this takes great self-discipline, but he must not get away with a bad habit even once.

- Seek advice, but if you know the horse well, pay attention to your gut feelings, too.

- Help the horse to confront any fears by exposing him to them as often as possible.

- Don't be too quick to blame the horse when things go wrong – there are more problem owners than problem horses.

- If a horse's behaviour causes you to lose confidence, pass him on to someone more suitable sooner rather than later.

- Look on every problem as an opportunity to learn and strengthen your relationship with your horse.

confidence. So when the horse returns, mutual trust will inevitably be at a very low ebb – yet this is just when they need a confident relationship to get off to a fresh start together. Putting the partnership back on a firm footing is essential if behavioural problems are to be treated successfully once and for all.

As any rider knows, horses only remain on their best behaviour for so long before testing out a new handler or situation, and handlers must discipline themselves as well as the horse. It is tempting to drop the tough act from time to time, and take the easier option of giving in to the horse – but this really isn't fair. Horses like to know where the limits are, and life is in fact a lot easier when he understands that 'no' means 'no', not 'maybe'. Therefore think black and white every time you handle your horse, and don't allow any grey areas to creep in.

As well as trying to understand your horse's psychology and body language a little better in order to prevent the problem recurring, be honest about your own abilities. Could it have been insensitive riding or incorrect handling that caused the problem in the first place? Until the owner is cured, neither is the horse.

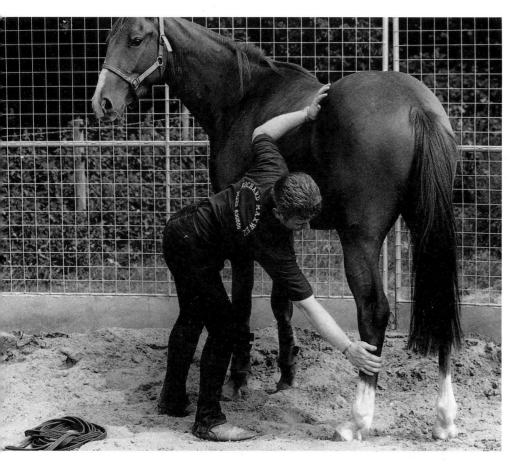

◀ Handling the horse's vulnerable areas re-establishes his trust and confidence. As a flight animal, he finds it particularly difficult to 'disable' himself by standing on three legs, so picking up a foot for you is a real concession

▼ The loins are another sensitive area, vulnerable to predators in the wild

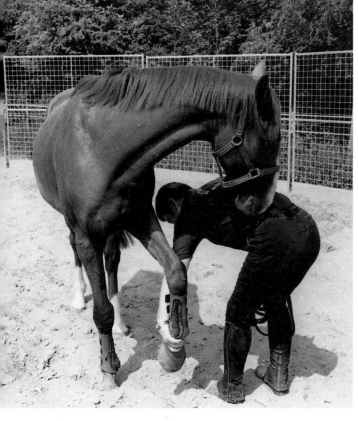

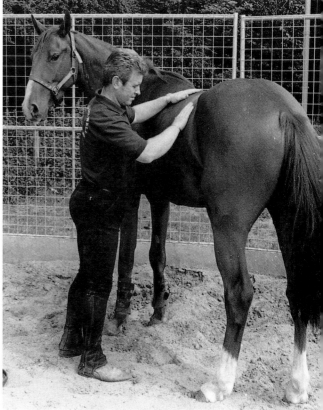

◀ Logical and reasonable handling is the key to problem-solving. This horse was head-shy and generally spooky, so we forced him to confront his fears by hanging brightly coloured bags and rustling bits of paper at head height around his stable. He couldn't move without bumping into them! It took him a full day to pluck up the courage to go near his feed and water – but to my mind it is worse to allow a horse to go on being terrified of having anything around his head when you can solve that problem for him and make him realise his mistake; he will be much happier for it in the long term

▼ Hanging feed bags in the stable desensitises a spooky horse

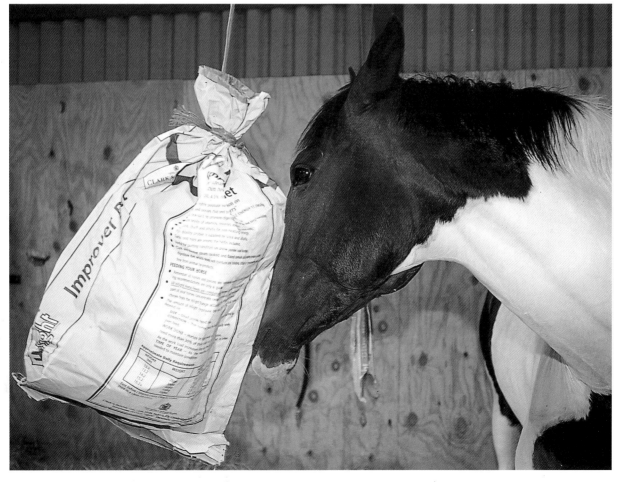

COMMON PROBLEMS & SOLUTIONS

RIDING

People always say you should be very experienced before taking on a youngster. How much experience is enough?

Max replies: Time, patience, common sense and intelligent, sympathetic handling can make up for a lack of experience. Anyone can have fun with a youngster if they are confident around older horses and have a good support network in terms of help and advice. However, if you have any doubts about your experience, you will find it easier to make progress with a youngster which has a naturally confident and laid-back attitude and has been well handled since birth.

Should I invest in a good saddle for my youngster straight away or will an old one do for breaking?

Max replies: If you must, use an old saddle for a couple of days only. As soon as the horse is backed and the rider starts spending more time on board, it is of the utmost importance to use a well-fitting saddle. The horse must never be made to feel uncomfortable by the equipment he wears, or he will be reluctant to go forward and do as he is asked, and will naturally associate discomfort with you. Resentment and tension will build up until you have a real problem on your hands. At this early stage of a horse's life, it is more

▲ The Reactorpanel saddle (*Your Horse* magazine)

important than ever that every ridden experience is a positive one. As the horse grows and changes shape, you are likely to have to change his saddle too, but this is a necessary expense which you must budget for when buying a young horse. Buying second-hand or borrowing from friends may be an option; I always use Reactorpanel saddles, which can be refitted as the horse changes shape.

What is the best way to introduce a youngster to jumping? In the arena with poles, or out on a hack?

Max replies: The first step is to introduce the horse to poles in-hand, leading him in a headcollar initially and later long-reining over them.

◀ A spirited youngster: will he be too much for you?

▲ Accustom your youngster to trotting over coloured poles with confidence before attempting any jumping (*Your Horse* magazine)

If you can then find a suitable enclosed area with a good surface, loose jumping is an excellent way for a youngster to get used to jumping without the hindrance of a rider's weight. The fences should be kept small so that he gains confidence and feels the whole experience is fun, not stressful.

If you have done the groundwork and your youngster is balanced and responsive on the flat in walk, trot and canter with a rider, there is no reason why you cannot move quickly onto jumping small fences in the arena from time to time. Cross poles are good fences to start with, as they are inviting and encourage the horse to jump in the middle. As the horse's confidence and balance grow, so can the fences!

It is not a good idea to introduce jumping out on a hack because all youngsters will make mistakes as they learn to jump. If he hits one, not only will the fences be solid, thus punishing him unfairly for his boldness, but you may fall off and turn the whole experience into a

rather frightening, negative one. As soon as you are both jumping well in the arena, by all means try small obstacles out on a hack as long as there is someone with you.

What are the pros and cons of using a crop versus a schooling whip?

Max replies: I wouldn't use either with a youngster. I would use what I call an Over and Under (see page 106). This is flicked behind the rider's leg from one side of the horse to the other in a pendulum motion, to create forward movement without pain or confusion. The movement of the rope across the horse's withers makes it psychologically uncomfortable for him to stay still, as he can see the movement on both sides. As soon as the horse moves forward, cease using it until you feel the horse 'thinking backwards' again.

When I take my young horse out on the road, he shies a lot at unfamiliar objects such as pub signs and gateways. How can I train him to pass such objects safely?

▲ Calm and collected (*Your Horse* magazine)

Max replies: You shouldn't really take your young horse out on the road until he understands and respects the leg aids. If you approach something and feel the horse starting to shy, turn his head away from the object which is frightening him and ask him to go forward. Do not allow him to become fixated with whatever is worrying him. Practise leg yielding in the manège; you will be surprised how much this will help you in such situations on the road.

My three-year-old cob is very strong and I have problems stopping him in canter. His previous owner rode him in an eggbutt jointed snaffle. What is the best approach – to upgrade his bit or improve his manners?

Mac replies: Have his teeth checked by a qualified equine dentist, as the horse's mouth is going through a great deal of change at this age. He will need more frequent check-ups until he is about five, and has a full set of adult teeth.

If all is well in his mouth, go back to establishing obedience to the aids. Use half halts and plenty of

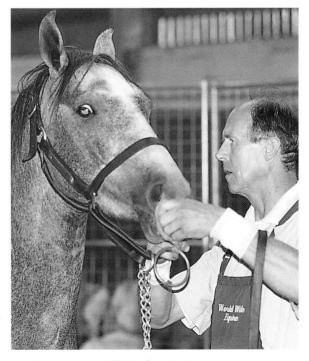

▲ Always use a qualified equine dentist

transitions and changes of direction to get him off his forehand, improve his balance and stop him leaning on you. If he gets tired he is even more likely to fall onto his forehand, so keep sessions short and sweet.

A youngster's natural inclination is to be on the forehand until he is trained to collect and transfer weight backwards onto the haunches, and a stronger bit will not cure this. At just three years old, he should be ridden in the mildest bit possible.

Is it good for a youngster to have different people on board or will it confuse him? I'd rather be the only one to ride my four-year-old, but a friend has suggested it would be good for his education to be ridden by others.

Max replies: You are both right! Initially it will help your horse's confidence to have one person riding him, and will also ensure that he is ridden and handled consistently in the early stages, when he is trying hard to understand what is required of him.

◀ 'Who's this?' Allowing a competent friend to ride him will help to broaden your youngster's education (*Your Horse* magazine)

▲ Experienced help from the ground is invaluable with a young horse (*Your Horse* magazine)

Once the basics are established, however, it is an important part of the youngster's education to be ridden by others, provided that they are confident, competent and sympathetic riders.

Everyone has their own way of doing things, so it will also help iron out any peculiarities caused by your riding!

My young horse stumbles a lot when doing flat work. Why might he do this?

Max replies: Horses stumble for a number of reasons. They may be on the forehand, have over-long feet, a poorly balanced rider, badly fitting saddle or simply be weak and tired. You need to establish the cause for your horse's stumbling before you can effect a cure. Once you have eliminated the cause, go back to the manège and reschool.

Schooling is about quality, not quantity, and it always helps if you have someone to help you from the ground. You need to get your horse working from behind so that he is able to balance himself and reduce the chances of stumbling.

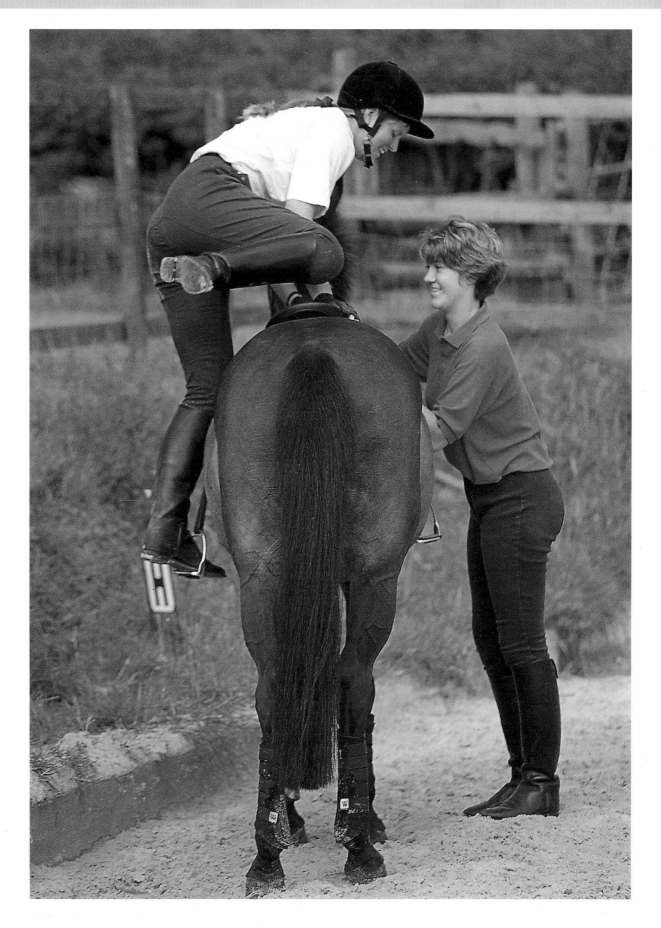

Pain or pleasure? The horse's expression and way of going will tell you the difference

My horse constantly walks off as I try to mount. If I correct him, he rears up and spins round. What's wrong?

Max replies: It sounds as if your horse has a dental problem (possibly a rear hook), or a trapped nerve in the poll area. Rearing and spinning are classic symptoms of either or both of these problems. Your horse reacts violently because you put him in a great deal of pain as you ask him to stop wandering off.

Once a qualified therapist and equine dentist have eliminated these physical problems as a cause of bad behaviour, you may find that your horse still behaves this way out of habit. School your horse to the pressure halter and teach him to stand still when asked, without a rider. Then you can put the pressure halter on underneath his bridle, and have someone ready to school him in the same way if he wanders off as you

mount. Alternatively, get somebody else to ride so that you can be on the ground schooling. As soon as he stands still release the pressure and praise him. It should only take a couple of sessions because horses learn quickly when presented with a clear positive and negative option.

My young horse rushes at fences. I thought it was enthusiasm, but my friend says it's the opposite, and that he is rushing to get it over with. What do you think?

Max replies: It could be either, and without seeing you and the horse I cannot tell. However, your friend is right in one respect – horses often rush at fences out of panic and a desire to get them over and done with. This could be because they are confused about what you really want, generally anxious about jumping after a previous

◀ Simple re-schooling should quickly stop any 'wandering off' tendency in your horse (*Your Horse* magazine)

bad experience or in some sort of physical pain made considerably worse by the physical exertion required when jumping. The horse's back, teeth and saddle should be checked by experts to give him the best chance of enjoying the job you are asking him to do. The longer you leave it, the more confirmed the horse will become in his belief that jumping is anything but fun.

How can I teach my novice horse to respond to my leg aids? I can't seem to make him bend or move laterally at all.

Max replies: I never have this problem, and I believe it is because of the amount of long-lining I do (see Stage 7) in preference to lungeing, which many people use extensively with youngsters. The long lines effectively take the place of the rider's legs and you can increase or decrease the pressure according to how the horse is responding. I long-line on a circle and include lots of turns and transitions, until the horse becomes really flexible and forward going.

I think the answer is to get your youngster properly established on long-lines, eventually refining it so that as well as moving forward from the lines he learns to move laterally too. Every time you ask him to move, make a clicking noise so that once you are riding again, you can coincide your leg aid with the same click until he learns to associate the two.

I have just started taking my young horse out on the roads for the first time. She behaves well when traffic approaches from the front, but is very jumpy when it overtakes us from behind. A friend has suggested putting on a closed bridle, as used by carriage drivers. Would this help build up her confidence?

Max replies: I wouldn't use a closed bridle. Instead, hang all sorts of plastic feed sacks, dangling ropes and other hazards from the roof of her stable, so that they brush against her as she moves around. This is a really good way to 'despook' a horse and get him used to noise and movement from behind, desensitising him without human intervention. Hang them so that she has to walk through them to get to her hay, water and feed, and that when she is eating they touch her behind. Don't be put off if she stands at the back of her box all day at first! She will eventually start to explore, and most horses eventually find them quite amusing and use them as playthings.

HANDLING

What do I do if my youngster leans his weight on me when I pick up his foot?

Max replies: The reason your youngster is leaning on you is because he feels unsure and worried by what you are asking him to do. You need to go back and start again, asking a little at a time and not expecting your youngster to hold his foot up for too long. Make sure that he is standing square before you start, so that he has more chance of remaining balanced when you take

▲ Youngsters are naturally curious of anything new – especially if it's something chewable! (*Your Horse* magazine)

the foot away. Don't try to support the horse by leaning back into him – it will make the problem worse (see 'Into pressure' on page 41).

My youngster has never worn a rug before. What's the best way to introduce it without frightening him?

Max replies: I would start with a summer sheet, or something lightweight which doesn't rustle too much. Don't attempt to put it straight on his back – allow your youngster to have a good sniff and even paw and

mouth at the rug if he wants to. When he is familiar with the material, quietly but positively throw it over his back. It is important not to be sneaky about this, thinking you can prevent him from jumping – he's more likely to do that if you sneak up on him, and you will also give the impression that it is something worth worrying about! If your youngster seems happy then build on this until you can take it on and off without a problem, then move onto heavier rugs.

If he seems unduly worried, then hang the rug from the ceiling which will allow him to get used to the feel of it brushing over his back without human intervention.

My horse loads relatively easily, but panics and kicks out when the ramp is raised. I have tried getting someone to stand behind with a stick to encourage him forwards and stop him running back, but the problem seems to be getting worse.

Max replies: The worst thing you can do with a horse who refuses to load or worries about the ramp going up behind him is to smack him with a whip. Far from encouraging him forward, he becomes even more preoccupied with what is going on behind him and feels

the need to kick out or run back to defend himself. As a flight animal, his first option would be to run away, but the lorry ramp denies him this course of action so he is forced to resort to other methods in order to save himself from what he perceives to be a threatening situation. The horse's sense of self-preservation is very strong, which is why the species has survived its many predators for so long. When trying to load him, you must respect this flight instinct but reassure the horse through firm but sympathetic handling that travelling is nothing to worry about.

At the moment he equates the lorry with an unpleasant, uncomfortable situation, which you have confirmed by smacking him just as he is trying to overcome his fear and do the right thing! You need to go back to basics with a pressure halter (see pages 131–2), and once the horse is inside the lorry make him realise that staying in and backing out calmly is as big a discipline as loading. Rather than whips, get somebody to pat and stroke his quarters when he is in the box, to reassure him that he has nothing to worry about from behind. For safety, your helper should wear a hard hat and stand well to one side. Details of my

▼ This horse is starting to walk up the ramp, albeit reluctantly, but the owner has unwisely drawn his attention backwards towards the ever-ready stick. Not surprisingly, the horse reacts violently to this unprovoked attack from behind. Such treatment increases the horse's anxiety about the loading business and is unlikely to induce him to co-operate

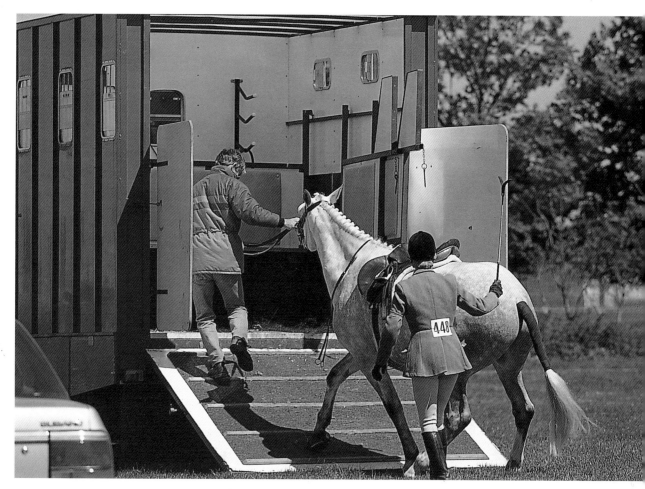

video 'Solving loading problems', which tells you how to deal with this very problem, are on page 150.

My horse is fine to load and travels well, but barges his way out of the lorry at the other end, virtually jumping down the ramp.

Max replies: This comes down to the fact that your horse has no respect for you as a handler, and has become deliberately forgetful about the area of personal space which surrounds you. It is not acceptable for horses to barge their handlers, and it will result in injury to you or him sooner or later.

No doubt this lack of respect is reflected in other areas of his training too, perhaps in his stable manners, although you see him at his worst when coming out of the lorry. A properly halter-broken horse remains conscious of his manners and the 'bubble' of personal space around the handler regardless of the situation. Before you take him back into the lorry, you need to re-establish his respect for you on the ground. Refer back to Stage 3 on halter-breaking, and use the pressure halter to get him

listening to you. Once you have his attention he should show signs of 'reading' your body language and responding to it more readily, rather than ignoring you. Take him back into the box and start again, this time being ready to school bad behaviour using your body language and the pressure halter until he has overcome this habit.

My horse picks up his foot easily, but then snatches it away. I can't hang on to it: what should I do?

Max replies: Initially, a young horse may snatch his foot away because he feels unbalanced and insecure, and is worried about falling over. This is understandable at first, but it can become habitual, so that even when he is quite capable of standing on three legs the horse still snatches the foot away rather than waiting for you to let go. It is very difficult and not really advisable to hang on to the leg, so it's easy for the horse to end up getting his own way.

Make sure he is completely comfortable about having his legs handled in the first place, and that he is

standing square and balanced before you start. Don't ask him to hold the foot up for too long, to give you the chance to put it down before he snatches. Reward positive behaviour immediately, and build on this principle until you can hold the foot up for longer periods.

I would like to keep my colt entire: what are your thoughts? If he is to be gelded, when is the best time to do it?

Max replies: Keeping entires is a major responsibility and takes dedication and hard work. The most important factor is where the horse is to be kept, as there are obvious stable management problems if you intend to turn him out near mares, for example. Most people's perception of entires is that they are nasty and aggressive, so they either isolate and ignore them, tease them, or become excessively aggressive in their handling in the mistaken belief that the horse will respect them more for it, and that this will prevent him 'trying it on'.

On the contrary, entires are highly sociable and fun-loving creatures, and it is not natural for them to be segregated. The frustration of living in such a situation may well lead to the type of behaviour you are trying to avoid. If you can provide firm, fair handling and are prepared for the extra time and dedication an entire needs, the rewards can be enormous because entires are such loyal and intelligent creatures to work with. If not, it is advisable to have him cut shortly after weaning, preferably when there are no flies about.

BEHAVIOUR

My horse is headshy. Is there anything other than gentle persuasion which might help?

Max replies: On page 133 you will see a picture of a horse with all kinds of 'hazards' hanging over his manger and around the box. Exposing the horse to his fears and making him confront them in this way is a good start. Handling the head sympathetically but firmly is the next step. Do not allow yourself to be shaken off when you try to lay a hand on a headshy horse's face – keep it there until he realises you can't be pushed away like an irritating fly. When he stops trying to shake you off, then is the time to take your hand away, thus rewarding him for his positive reaction.

▶ Don't be put off keeping your colt entire: it can be a hugely rewarding experience, with good handling he should be well-disciplined enough to lead without the bit being used to exert control (*Your Horse* magazine)

Around the ears is usually the worst area for headshy horses, so as his confidence grows, work your hand higher and higher until you can fondle around the base and eventually the tips of the ears. This process should be repeated as often as possible, certainly once a day, and may take several weeks in really bad cases. Patience and persistence are the only cures.

My horse seems to hate men! Can this be cured?

Max replies: This is a fairly common complaint, although it is often in the owner's imagination, and I have rarely met a horse who truly dislikes men unless he has been severely beaten up by one. However, an uncomfortable experience with the vet or farrier may lead the horse to distrust men in some cases. The answer lies in exposing him to male company as much as possible, until the horse realises that he has nothing to fear. Make a point of asking every male who comes in or near the yard to talk to your horse and make a fuss of him, whether they are interested in horses or not!

ACKNOWLEDGEMENTS

My thanks go to Monty Roberts for opening my mind to the possibilities; my wife, Sam, for her support and hard work behind the scenes; Jo Sharples, who put my thoughts and beliefs into words; Bob Atkins, who understood what I was looking for and captured it on film; Lucy Emerick, Jo Charlwood and Kiara Lyons, who have taken care of the yard in my absence; Andy Andrews, a constant source of knowledge and advice; Barry Horne and Teresa Curtis, for allowing us to photograph their youngstock; and finally all the 'problem' horses who have proved this process to be a good one, and made this book necessary.

Richard Maxwell

To my mare Bon Espoir, who asked so many questions, and to Max and Marjorie Armstrong, who gave me the answers.

Jo Sharples

INDEX

Page references in *italic* indicate illustrations